Introduction to Computers

2020 Edition

By

Darrell Hajek,

Cesar Herrera

Preface:

In 2017 we learned that the prices of the texts used in our introductory computer literacy course had increased significantly (to over $150.) We felt that this was, not only excessive, but counterproductive, since very few students would be likely to buy the texts at that price.

We looked for alternative texts for the course but found none that we considered adequate for both content and price, and so, we decided to write our own.

We have tried to include all of the material necessary for an introductory course for computer literacy, but, in order to maintain a low price for our students, we have attempted to keep the content to ONLY what would be desirable for such a course. We fully expect that many will disagree with the choices we have made, both in what we have included and (probably even more) in what we have failed to include. We are revisiting these decisions as we prepare new editions annually. Suggestions and recommendations are welcome.

We have created a set of supplementary PowerPoint files, as well as testbanks. We will be happy to make both available to any teacher who has decided to adopt the book as assigned text for a course.

You are welcome to contact us at either darrell.hajek@upr.edu or cesar.herrera@upr.edu .

Contents

Contents

Contents

Contents

Contents

Contents

Contents

Contents

Contents

Contents

1 Introduction

Humans have always found it necessary to perform some kinds of calculations, and over the centuries, people have used many *devices* to perform these calculations. The complexity of these devices has been increasing as new needs have developed with the progress of technology.

The oldest known calculating device is the abacus[i], which was invented in Asia over 2,000 years ago.

Since the development of the abacus, calculating devices have been continuously refined, culminating with our modern digital computers. Today, computers play a very important role in solving a huge variety of problems. The modern uses of computers include: (among many others)

allowing calculations to be performed very quickly,

automating repetitive processes,

storing and manipulating large quantities of data,

allowing us to browse the Internet.

This chapter provides a review of the developments that resulted in the construction of the first computer. It also presents a brief description of the evolution of the computer from its origins until this century.

1.1 Evolution of the Computer:

1.1.1 Earliest Devices

Humans have been using different kinds of devices to help them do calculations since well before recorded history began.

Probably the first *calculating **aids*** people used were their *fingers*.

(but fingers would probably not be considered to be *devices* in the sense we would normally use the term.)

The earliest widely used mechanical calculating device, the [ii]abacus, was used by the Sumerians and Egyptians as early as 2000 BC. Its use was widespread among the Romans, Indians, Chinese and Japanese.

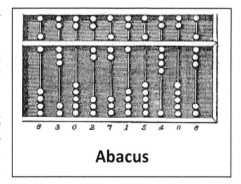

Abacus

Several kinds of analog computers were constructed in ancient and medieval times to perform astronomical calculations. These include the Antikythera mechanism[iii] and the astrolabe[iv], both developed in ancient Greece (c. 150–100 BC),

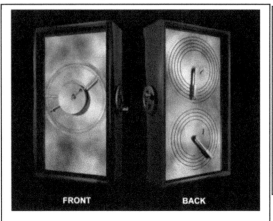

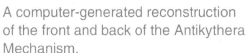

A computer-generated reconstruction of the front and back of the Antikythera Mechanism.

Astrolabe

1.1.2 1600's: Mechanical Calculators

Throughout the 17'th century there was a great deal of interest in designing and building mechanical calculators. Particularly noteworthy were the calculators designed and built by Blaise Pascal[v] and by Gottfried Leibnitz[vi] (who also described the binary number system that is used in all modern computers.) It was in this period that the slide rule[vii] first appeared (attributed, in part to Isaac Newton.)

Pascal's calculator

Leibnitz calculator

Slide Rule

1.1.3   1800's: Babbage

The next steps in the development of what we now think of as computers were taken by Charles Babbage during the 19'th century. Babbage first designed what he called his *difference engine*. The difference engine was designed to calculate values of polynomial functions. Babbage never succeeded in manufacturing a difference engine, although others made a few machines based on his designs. One of the reasons that he failed to make a working difference engine is that he turned his attention to a more advanced design which he called the

Babbage Analytical Engine

analytical engine[viii]. The analytical engine was, in fact, a programmable computer. The design for the analytical engine included many ideas that were later incorporated into widely used computers beginning in the 1940's. These concepts included the use of punched cards to input data and programs (a method being used in the 19'th century to control mechanical looms most famously the Jacquard loom.) The analytical engine incorporated an arithmetic logic unit and ability to control sequence of command execution by means of conditional branching and loops. It also included integrated memory. Babbage was never able to complete construction of any of his machines due to conflicts with his chief engineer and inadequate funding. It was not until the 1940s that the first general-purpose computers were actually built

1.1.4   1940's: Electromechanical and Electronic Computers

By the 1940's it was becoming clear that electronic devices could do computation faster than mechanical devices.

As is all too often the case in technological development, it was *war* that motivated (and funded) much of the development of the computers of the 1940's and 1950's.

The world's first programmable, electronic, digital computers were the Colossus computers, developed for British codebreakers during World War II to help in the cryptanalysis. The Colossus Mark 1 first became operational in Feb. 1944 and an improved (much faster) Colossus Mark 2[ix] first put into service in June 1944, just in time for the Normandy landings.

Colossus Mark 2 Computer

In the United States, ENIAC, the first general purpose, programmable computer was initially designed to compute artillery firing tables for the US army. ENIAC[x] was not completed until shortly after the war ended, but it was immediately put to use in the development of the hydrogen bomb.

ENIAC being programmed

1.1.5 1950's: Commercial Computers

The first commercial computers appeared in 1951.

In England, the Lyons Electronic Office (LEO I) was the first computer used for commercial business applications.

UNIVAC[xi] was the first commercially successful electronic computer produced in the United States.

The first electronic computers were electromechanical, using electrical relays, but soon the electromechanical relays were replaced by vacuum tubes.

In 1947, the transistor was developed, and, beginning in about 1955 it began to be used in computers, resulting in smaller units that required less power and generated less heat. In 1957 the integrated circuit was developed, which shortly began resulting in even smaller units requiring even less power.

It was in the 1950's that IBM entered the computer business (which they were soon to completely dominate) starting with the [xii]IBM 650, the first mass-produced computer, with approximately 2000 installations.

[xiii]

LEO I

UNIVAC I

IBM 650

1.1.6 1960's and beyond:

Starting around 1960, the world's computing hardware began to very quickly convert from vacuum tube to solid state devices such as the transistor and, later, the integrated circuit. By 1959 discrete transistors were considered sufficiently reliable and economical that they made further vacuum tube computers uncompetitive. Computer main memory slowly moved away from magnetic core memory devices to solid-state semiconductor memory This greatly reduced the cost, size and power consumption of computing devices.

Eventually the cost of integrated circuit devices became low enough that home computers and personal computers were feasible.

With the introduction of the graphical user interface (GUI), the *use* of computers no longer required specialized training and the development of the Internet (especially the World Wide Web) allowed home and mobile computers (including smart phones) to be used for entertainment, finance (especially online banking), e-commerce (online shopping), personal research (Google search, Wikipedia), communications (e-mail, Instant Messaging, Facebook, Twitter) and education. Of course, with such widespread uses for such a wide range of people, there was a great proliferation of computers and computer applications that could not possibly have been imagined by the original pioneers in the field.

1.1.6.1 Artificial Intelligence

In computer science AI research is defined as the study of "intelligent agents": any device that perceives its environment and takes actions that maximize its chance of successfully achieving its goals. Colloquially, the term "artificial intelligence" is applied when a machine mimics "cognitive" functions that humans associate with other human minds, such as "learning" and "problem solving".

Modern machine capabilities generally classified as AI include successfully understanding human speech, competing at the highest level in strategic game systems (such as chess and Go), autonomously operating cars, and intelligent routing in content delivery networks and military simulations.

The traditional problems (or goals) of AI research include reasoning, knowledge representation, planning, learning, natural language processing, perception and the ability to move and manipulate objects. General intelligence is among the field's long-term goals.

Some people also consider AI will be a danger to humanity if it progresses unabated. Others believe that AI, unlike previous technological revolutions, will create a risk of mass unemployment.

1.1.6.2 Virtual Reality

Modern computing systems are being used more and more for implementation of *Virtual Reality* (VR)systems. Virtual reality (VR) is an experience taking place within a simulated environment. Such an environment can be similar to the real world, but might also be completely different from the real world.

Applications of virtual reality include entertainment (i.e. gaming) but it also enjoys wide use for educational purposes (i.e. medical or military training.)

[xiv]Currently, most virtual reality systems use either virtual reality headsets or multi-projected environments to generate realistic images, sounds and other sensations that simulate a user's physical presence in a virtual environment.

A person using virtual reality equipment is able to look around the artificial world, move around in it, and interact with virtual features or items. The effect is commonly created by VR headsets consisting of a head-mounted display with a small screen in front of the eyes.

Researcher with the European Space Agency in Darmstadt, Germany, equipped with a HTC Vive VR headset and motion controllers

Virtual reality effects can also be created with specially designed rooms having multiple large screens.

Virtual reality typically incorporates auditory and video feedback, but may also allow other types of sensory and force feedback through *haptic technology*.

1.1.6.2.1 Haptic Technology

[xv]Haptic technology (also known as kinesthetic communication or 3D touch) refers to technology that can create an experience of touch by applying forces, vibrations, or motions to the user. This mechanical stimulation can be used to create virtual objects in a computer simulation, to control such virtual objects, and to enhance the remote control of machines and devices (telerobotics).

A 1980s era head-mounted display and wired gloves at the NASA Ames Research Center

Haptic devices may also incorporate tactile sensors that measure forces exerted by the user on the interface. Several kinds of haptic devices are common in the form of game controllers, joysticks, and steering wheels.

1.1.7 Different classes of computers:

Starting around 1960, computer manufacturers began specializing – producing different types of computers aimed at specific segments of the market:

1.1.7.1 Mainframe computers

[xvi]Mainframe computers are computers used primarily by commercial and governmental organizations for critical applications and bulk data processing such as census, industry and consumer statistics, enterprise resource planning and transaction processing.

The term "Mainframe" originally referred to the large cabinets that housed the central processing unit and main memory of early computers. Later, the term was used to distinguish high-end commercial machines from less powerful units.

IBM has traditionally dominated this portion of the market. Their dominance grew out of their 700/7000 series and, later, the development of the 360 series mainframes.

An IBM 704 Installation

1.1.7.2 Minicomputers

Minicomputers are a class of smaller computers that developed in the mid-1960s and cost much less than the mainframe and mid-size computers from IBM.
When single-chip CPUs appeared, beginning with the Intel 4004 in 1971, the term "minicomputer" came to mean a machine that lies in the middle range of the computing spectrum, smaller than the mainframe computers but larger than the microcomputers. Minicomputers usually took up one or a few 19-inch rack cabinets.

Compare this with the large mainframes that could fill an entire room.

A PDP-8 on display at the Smithsonian's National Museum of American

The definition of *minicomputer* is vague, and, consequently, there are a number of candidates for being the **first** minicomputer. An early and highly successful minicomputer was Digital Equipment Corporation's (DEC) PDP-8[xvii], which was launched in 1964 and cost from US$16,000 upwards.

The term *minicomputer* is no longer widely used. The term *midrange computer* is now preferred.

1.1.7.3 Supercomputers

Supercomputers are computers that have world-class computational capacity. In 2015, such machines could perform quadrillions of floating point operations per second.

[xviii]Supercomputers were introduced in the 1960s, made initially, and for decades primarily by Seymour Cray at Control Data Corporation (CDC), then at Cray Research and at subsequent companies, all bearing his name or monogram.

CDC 6600

The first computer to be commonly referred to as a *supercomputer* was the CDC6600, released in 1964. It was designed by Cray and was the fastest in the world by a large margin. It demonstrated that there was a viable supercomputing market when one hundred computers were sold at $8 million each.

Cray left CDC in 1972 and formed his own company, Cray Research Inc. In 1976, Cray Research delivered the Cray-1[xix] which became one of the most successful supercomputers in history.

In Nov 2018, the IBM Summit at Oak Ridge National Laboratory became the fastest supercomputer in the world. Before Nov 2018, the two fastest machines were both in China. The Sunway TaihuLight at China's National Supercomputing Center in Wuxi, was fastest and second fastest was the Tianhe-2 at the National Supercomputer Center in Guangzho.

The US government has also contracted another (to be named Frontier) designed to be 50 times faster than Summit. Frontier is scheduled for completion in 2021.

Cray-1 preserved at the Deutsches Museum

As of 2019, China has 227 supercomputers while the US has 109. Supercomputers are used in a wide range of computationally intensive tasks in various fields, including quantum mechanics, weather forecasting, climate research, oil and gas exploration, molecular modeling (computing the structures and properties of chemical compounds, biological macromolecules, polymers, and crystals), and physical simulations (such as simulations of the early moments of the universe, airplane and spacecraft aerodynamics, the detonation of nuclear weapons, and nuclear fusion). Throughout their history, they have been essential in the field of cryptanalysis.

1.1.7.4 Personal Computers

Personal computers are general-purpose computers whose size, capabilities and original sale price make them viable for individuals. They are intended to be operated directly by end-users with no intervening computer operators.

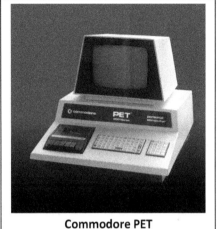

Early personal computers (generally called *microcomputers*) were often sold in a kit form, in limited volumes, and were of interest mostly to hobbyists and technicians.

The first successfully mass marketed personal computer was the Commodore PET[xx], introduced in January 1977. At roughly the same time, the Apple II came out in June 1977, and the TRS-80, from Tandy Corporation / Tandy Radio Shack, in summer 1977.

Commodore PET

Mass-market ready-assembled computers allowed a wider range of people to use computers, many of whom began focusing more on software applications and less on development of the computer hardware.

In 1981, IBM announced their IBM Personal Computer (PC)[xxi]. Although not necessarily the best machine by technological standards, IBM's reputation (and marketing expertise) soon brought the PC to a position of dominance in the personal computer market.

The personal computer market soon split into two distinct types of computers:

IBM PC 5150.

Desktop computers: For a long time, desktop computers were the most common type of personal computer. These are characterized by being small enough to fit on top of (or beside or beneath) a desk. A typical desktop computer requires an external power source, since they are normally used in locations (homes, offices, …) where external power is readily available. Internal batteries would be an unnecessary expense.

Laptop Computers: Also called *portable* computers or *notebook* computers, as well as various other names.

A laptop can be powered either from a rechargeable battery, or by household electricity via an AC adapter.

"*Laptop*" is a diverse category of devices and many more specific terms, such as "rugged notebook" or "convertible", refer to specialist types of laptops, which have been optimized for specific uses. Hardware specifications

Laptop Computer

change significantly between different types, makes and models of laptops.

Laptop computers have developed to the point that they have essentially the same capabilities as desktop computers. They are, however, a little more expensive and cannot be upgraded as easily.

1.1.7.5 PDA's

As technology evolved, it became possible to make computers small enough to hold in one hand, and the portable computer merged with the pocket calculator to become what was often referred to as a **personal digital assistant,** or **PDA.**

A PDA is a mobile device that functions as a personal information manager. PDAs were discontinued in early 2010s after the widespread adoption of smartphones and tablets.

The term *PDA* first appeared in January 1992, referring to the *Apple Newton*.[xxii]

In 1994, IBM introduced the IBM Simon[xxiii], which was the first PDA with full mobile phone functionality. The IBM Simon can also be considered the first smartphone.

In 1996, Nokia introduced a PDA with full mobile phone functionality, the 9000 Communicator, which became the world's best-selling PDA. The Communicator spawned a new category of PDAs: the "*PDA phone*", now called "smartphone". Another early entrant in this market was Palm[xxiv], with a line of PDA products which began in March 1996.

Palm TX

Apple Newton and I-Phone

IBM Simon and charging base

1.1.7.6 Smartphones[xxv]

Smartphones typically combine the features of a cell phone with those of other popular mobile devices, such as personal digital assistant, media player and GPS navigation unit. It is the mobile phone functionality that distinguishes the smart phone from the PDA. Most smartphones have a touchscreen user interface, can run third-party apps, and have cameras built in.

Smartphones

1.1.7.7 Tablet Computers

The smartphone proved to be too small for many uses and, starting around 1910, the *"tablet computer"* emerged as a device intermediate in size between a smartphone and a laptop.

> A **tablet computer** is a mobile computer with a touchscreen display, circuitry and battery in a single unit.

Tablets come equipped with cameras, microphones and accelerometers. The touchscreen display uses finger or stylus gestures substituting for the use of mouse and keyboard in a standard personal computer. Tablets usually feature on-screen, pop-up virtual keyboards for typing.

Tablets may include physical buttons for basic features such as speaker volume and power. They also typically have ports for network communications and battery charging.

Tablets are typically larger than smartphones or personal digital assistants.

iPad

The first modern tablet, the iPad[xxvi], was released in 2010.

1.1.7.8 Embedded Computers

The reduction in size, price and power consumption of computer components has made it possible to install specialized computers as embedded systems in many devices.

Embedded systems are generally designed to do some specific task, rather than be a general-purpose computer for multiple tasks. Some also have specific constraints for reasons such as safety and usability. Others may have low performance requirements, allowing the system hardware to be simplified to reduce costs.

Embedded systems are installed in things that range from portable devices, such as digital watches and MP3 players, to large stationary installations like traffic lights, factory controllers, and large complex systems like hybrid vehicles.

1.1.7.9 Smart TV's

Computing capability has also been built into the home TV set creating the *"Smart TV"*. This gives the advantage of a much larger viewing screen than found on the typical desktop computer. (Of course it lacks the portability of the laptop, smartphone and tablet.)

Smart TVs, much like smartphones and other smart home devices, offer internet connectivity and they support a range of apps. This allows users to watch movies and shows when they want to (streaming) rather than when they happen to be broadcast.

They also opens up a world of new entertainment options, from streaming video to playing games, checking social media, and controlling a whole house full of connected gadgets. Smart TV's use apps to connect to websites like Youtube, Netflix, Hulu or Vimeo. Web browsers, which are generally included, can access social sites like Facebook and Twitter. Users can pair wireless keyboards, smartphones or tablets for input, making the smart TV almost as user-friendly as a PC for web browsing.

1.1.8 Communications and Networks

With increased use of computers, it became important to move data from one computer to another quickly and efficiently. This, then, motivated the development of computer *networks*.

A computer network, (or simply a network,) is a collection of computers and other hardware components (printers, modems, routers, …) interconnected by communication channels that allow sharing of resources and information. The individual entities connected to the network are referred to as *nodes*.

Computer networks come in many different sizes:

At one extreme is the home and small business local area network (*LAN*) which allows a few computers to copy information from one to another, and to share access to resources such as printers and modems for Internet access.

At the other extreme is the *Internet* which connects millions of users worldwide.

There are two general *types* of computer networks: *client-server networks* and *peer to peer networks*

1.1.8.1 Client-server networks

A **client-server** network employs only two types of nodes: *clients* and *servers*.

A **client** is a computer used by a user to connect to a network and make requests to servers.

A **server** is a computer that receives and responds to requests from client machines. The *server* provides *services* to *clients*, usually by sending information of some kind or receiving and processing information of some kind.

1.1.8.2 Peer to peer networks

Another type of network is known as **peer-to-peer**, because each node can simultaneously act as both a client and a server (unlike specialized servers of the **client-server** model) and because each has equivalent responsibilities and status.

Peer-to-peer architectures are often abbreviated using the acronym **P2P**.

1.1.8.3 Internet of Things

Many embedded systems connect and exchange data. This creates opportunities for more direct integration of the physical world into computer-based systems. It results in efficiency improvements, economic benefits, and reduced human exertions. This network of physical devices, vehicles, home appliances, and other items embedded with electronics, software, sensors, actuators, with connectivity through the internet, has come to be called the "Internet of Things".

The Internet of Things has expanded Internet connectivity beyond standard devices, such as desktops, laptops, smartphones and tablets, and includes any range of traditionally *dumb* or non-internet-enabled physical devices and everyday objects. Embedded with technology, these devices can communicate and interact over the Internet, and they can be remotely monitored and controlled. The Internet of Things also includes driverless vehicles, a branch of the Internet application that has recently started to gain a great deal of attention

1.1.8.4 VideoTelephony

The improvement in communication speed has enabled the development of visual. As well as audio communication.

VideoTelephony/Videoconferencing can enable individuals in distant locations to participate in meetings on short notice, with time and money savings. Technology such as VoIP can be used in conjunction with desktop videoconferencing to enable low-cost face-to-face meetings without leaving homes or desks, especially for businesses or schools with widespread offices or large or multiple campuses. The technology is also used for telecommuting, in which employees work from home. One research report based on a sampling of 1,800 corporate employees showed that, as of June 2010, 54% of the respondents with access to video conferencing used it "all of the time" or "frequently"

1.1.8.5 Virtual Private Networks

As computers started becoming ubiquitous, many businesses began connecting their computers and computing equipment in *private* local area networks.

The use of private computer networks provides numerous benefits[1], but it is extremely expensive to implement a private network covering an area larger than a single building. If a business were to utilize traveling salesmen, roaming representatives, or branch offices, it would be impossible to construct a private network connecting all of its users/nodes. In order for such businesses to enjoy the benefits of private networking systems for implementing *virtual* private networks (VPN's) were developed.

These systems make use of *public* networks (usually the Internet) for communications but give the appearance/impression to the users of working on a *private* local network.

---

[1]   If they didn't provide benefits, nobody would use them.

1.2 Computer Definition:

Although computers have their origins in mechanical calculating devices (primarily numerical calculators) they have been adapted to the processing of other kinds of data (text, sound, graphical, video, ...)

Thus, a computer is no longer simply a calculating device, but has evolved into a *data processing* device.

In order for the computer to *process* data, the data must be *available* in the computer to *be* processed. Further, the computer must have the ability to *access* the data and, then, to do something with it.

A computer is controlled by sequence of *commands*

Such a sequence of computer commands is called a *program*.

A computer must have both a *processor* and *memory*:

Processor: (often called a *Central Processing Unit* or **CPU**) is a device which actually *does* the data processing. For every possible action of the processor, there is a numerical code (called a machine command) which can be stored in the memory of the computer.

Memory: a place where the data (and machine commands controlling the actions of the CPU) can be stored.

1.2.1 Information Processing Cycle

A computer works by continually repeating four actions over and over:

Fetch:
The processor reads (*fetches*) a machine command from memory.

Decode:
The processor identifies the command action.

Execute:
The processor performs the action.

Store:
If the action resulted in the computation of some value, then that value is stored in an appropriate location.

In fact, the individual actions of a CPU tend to be very simple (add two numbers, copy a number from one memory location to another, ...) A computer derives its power not from the ability to perform powerful/complex actions, but rather from sheer speed, from being able to perform many simple actions in a very short period of time.

1.2.2 Hardware and Software

The terms *hardware* and *software* are frequently used with respect to computers and computer systems.

Hardware refers to the physical (electric, electronic, and mechanical) components of the system.

Software refers to the computer programs that control what the system does.

1.2.3 Artificial Neural Network

The Artificial Neural Network (ANN) is a relatively modern alternative implementation of computing functions.

A **neural network** is a network or circuit of (possibly artificial) neurons, or nodes. Thus, a neural network is either a biological neural network, made up of real biological neurons, or an artificial neural network, for solving artificial intelligence (AI) problems.

Unlike von Neumann model computations, artificial neural networks do not separate memory and processing. They operate via the flow of signals through the net connections, somewhat akin to biological networks.

These artificial networks may be used for predictive modeling, adaptive control and applications where they can be "*trained*". Self-learning resulting from experience can occur within networks, which can derive conclusions from a complex and seemingly unrelated set of information

1.3 Social Effects of Computers

The wide availability of affordable computing and communications technology has caused a number of major shifts in the way that society operates. They have changed, among other things, the way most of us work, the way we interact with each other and the ways we teach our children.

1.3.1 Effects in the workplace

Computing technology has greatly increased productivity and has greatly improved efficiency in the workplace. They have, however, placed greater responsibilities on the work force. Workers are required to USE those computers, and this means they have to know HOW to use them. *Computer literacy*, then, has become an important component of the skill set necessary for employability in the 21'st century.

Even jobs that do not require the use of computing technology are often advertised online, and many require that applicants *apply* online.

With widespread availability of computer communication, many jobs that previously required the worker be physically present in the place of work can now be done from home. A work arrangement in which employees do not commute or travel (e.g. by bus or car) to a central place of work, is called *telecommuting*. Many workers are also expected to be available to respond to phone, email or text messaging at all hours, and even during vacations.

According to a Reuters poll, approximately "one in five workers around the globe, telecommute frequently (particularly employees in the Middle East, Latin America and Asia), and nearly 10 percent work from home every day.

Computing and communications technology have also made it possible for many jobs to be done from other countries, often countries where wages are lower. This phenomenon of transferring jobs to other countries is known as *outsourcing*.

1.3.2 Social Interactions

Computer networking, and the Internet in particular, has created greatly enhanced communication capabilities.

One consequence of this enhanced communication capability is the phenomenon of online shopping. The ability to compare, and purchase goods online results in a much greater quantity and quality of goods available for anyone than ever before.

Another consequence is the expansion of *social networking* (the practice of expanding the number of one's business and/or social contacts by making connections through individuals, often through social media sites such as Facebook, Twitter, LinkedIn and Google+.)

Social networking can be a form of entertainment. It is great for meeting people with similar interests, and is definitely useful for staying in touch with old friends/acquaintances. It can also be a very effective promotional tool for businesses, entrepreneurs, writers, actors, musicians, or artists.

1.3.3 Political Effects

The rise of social networking has had an enormous effect on politics, especially in the US, but also increasingly elsewhere.

Barack Obama made effective use of Facebook and YouTube, both for fundraising and for promoting his positions and policies.

Donald Trump has become famous (notorious?) for his use of Twitter to promote his views and "rally his base"

1.3.4 Effects in Education

The effects on education due to computing technology can hardly be overstated. Many excellent educational software programs exist to help children learn. Educational games, as well as a variety of other programs, can help improve a child's skill in a number of different critical areas, including vocabulary, mathematics, logical thinking, typing, history, and many more. Computers also change the way children are educated at school. The Internet provides students with a wealth of extra resources for knowledge and research, in addition to their textbooks. Children who use computers and the Internet at an early age have a tendency to do better in class than those who don't.

As noted earlier, computer literacy is becoming an essential skill, both socially and for employment. Unfortunately, many children (and adults) have less access to computers and computing technology than do others. This *digital divide* in classes of people, those who have access and those who don't, has important consequences for society.

1.3.5 Hacking and Malware

Unfortunately, the widespread use of computers and communications technology has given new avenues of attack to those who wish to take advantage of us or to do us harm. We now have to protect our children (and ourselves) against cyberbullying, our computers must be protected against malware and businesses (as well as individuals) must go to great lengths to protect their systems against attacks by "hackers".[2]

'Malware' is a term used to refer to a variety of forms of hostile or intrusive software, including computer viruses, worms, Trojan horses, ransomware, spyware, adware, scareware, and other malicious programs. Malware is often disguised as, or embedded in, non-malicious files.

As of 2011, the majority of active malware threats were worms or Trojans rather than viruses

Malware is often used to gain information such as personal identification numbers or details, bank or credit card numbers, and passwords. If left unprotected, personal and networked computers can be at considerable risk against these threats, and so our computers are often defended by various types of protection elements, including firewalls, anti-virus software, and various kinds of network hardware.

1.3.6 Computer Forensics

Starting in the early 1980's, the increased accessibility of personal computers began to lead to their increased use in criminal activity. The discipline of computer forensics emerged during this time as a method to recover and investigate digital evidence for use in court. Since then computer forensics has become more and more important, as computer crime and computer related crime have continued to increase. Computer forensics is used to investigate a wide variety of crime, including child pornography, fraud, espionage, cyberstalking, murder and rape. The discipline is also frequently used in civil proceedings as a form of information gathering.

---

[2] The term **hacker** was once used to describe a computer expert who used his technical knowledge to overcome a problem. It has come, in the popular culture, to be used to describe someone who uses his technical knowledge to break into computer systems.

1.4 Questions:

1.4.1 Completion

1. Humans have always found it necessary to perform some kinds of calculations, and over the centuries, people have used many _____ to perform these calculations

1. The oldest known calculating device is the _____ which was invented in Asia over 2000 years ago.

1.1.1 Several kinds of analog computers were constructed in ancient and medieval times to perform astronomical calculations. These include the Antikythera mechanism and the _____, both developed in ancient Greece (c. 150–100 BC)

1.1.4 The world's first programmable, electronic, digital computers were the _____ computers, developed for British codebreakers during World War II to help in the cryptanalysis

1.1.4 In the United States, _____, the first general purpose, programmable computer was initially designed to compute artillery firing tables for the US army

1.1.7 Starting around _____, computer manufacturers began specializing – producing different types of computers aimed at specific segments of the market:

1.1.7.1 _____ computers are computers used primarily by commercial and governmental organizations for critical applications and bulk data processing such as census, industry and consumer statistics, enterprise resource planning and transaction processing

1.1.7.1 The term "_____" originally referred to the large cabinets that housed the central processing unit and main memory of early computers. Later, the term was used to distinguish high-end commercial machines from less powerful units

1.1.7.2 The term *minicomputer* is no longer widely used. The term _____ *computer* is now preferred

1.1.7.3 The first computer to be commonly referred to as a *supercomputer* was the _____, released in 1964.

1.1.7.3 Supercomputers were introduced in the 1960s, made initially, and for decades primarily by Seymour _____ at Control Data Corporation (CDC), then at subsequent companies, all bearing his name or monogram

1.1.7.5 A(n) _____ is a mobile device that functions as a personal information manager. They were discontinued in early 2010s after the widespread adoption of smartphones and tablets.

1.1.7.7 A(n) _____ **computer** is a mobile computer with a touchscreen display, circuitry and battery in a single unit

1.1.7.7 The first modern tablet, the _____, was released in 2010

1.1.8 With increased use of computers it became important to move data from one computer to another quickly and efficiently. This, then, motivated the development of computer _____

1.1.8 There are many different sizes and types of networks. At one extreme is the _____ which allows a few computers to copy information from one to another, and to share access to resources such as printers and modems for Internet access.

1.1.8.1 A(n) _____ is a computer used by a user to connect to a network and make requests to servers.

1.1.8.1 A(n) _____ is a computer that receives and responds to requests from client machines

1.2 A computer is controlled by sequence of machine commands. Such a sequence of computer commands is called a(n) _____

1.3.4 The term _____ was once used to describe a computer expert who used his technical knowledge to overcome a problem. It has come, in the popular culture, to be used to describe someone who uses his technical knowledge to break into computer systems.

1.3.5 Starting in the early 1980's, the increased accessibility of personal computers began to lead to their increased use in criminal activity. The discipline of computer _____ emerged during this time as a method to recover and investigate digital evidence for use in court.

1.4.2 Multiple Choice

1. The oldest known calculating device is the abacus which was invented in _____over 2000 years ago.
   a) Asia
   b) Rome
   c) India
   d) Greece
   e) none of the above

1.1.1 The astrolabe, a kind of analog computer, was developed in ancient _____
   a) India
   b) China
   c) Greece
   d) Egypt
   e) none of the above)

1.1.2 _____ described the binary number system that is used in all modern computers
   a) Pascal
   b) Leibnitz
   c) Newton
   d) Lovelace
   e) none of the above

1.1.3 _____ designed the *analytical engine*, which was, in fact, a programmable computer. The design for the analytical engine included many ideas that were later incorporated into widely used computers beginning in the 1940's
   a) Pascal
   b) Leibnitz
   c) Newton
   d) Lovelace
   e) none of the above

1.1.4 _____ was the world's first programmable, electronic, digital computer
   a) Colossus Mark 1
   b) ENIAC
   c) LEO 1
   d) UNIVAC
   e) none of the above

1.1.5 _____ was the first computer used for commercial business applications
   a) Colossus Mark 1
   b) ENIAC
   c) LEO 1
   d) UNIVAC
   e) none of the above

1.1.5 _____ was the first mass-produced computer, with approximately 2000 installations.
a) Colossus Mark 1
b) ENIAC
c) LEO 1
d) UNIVAC
e) none of the above

1.1.5 It was in the _____'s that IBM entered the computer business
a) 1920
b) 1930
c) 1940
d) 1950
e) none of the above

1.1.6 During the 1960's
a) the world's computing hardware began to convert from vacuum tube to solid state devices
b) computer main memory moved away from magnetic core memory devices to solid-state semiconductor memory
c) with the introduction of the graphical user interface (GUI), the *use* of computers no longer required specialized training
d) all of the above
e) none of the above

1.1.7.4 The first successfully mass marketed personal computer was the _____
a) Apple II
b) TRS-80
c) Commodore PET
d) IBM PC
e) none of the above

1.1.7.5 The term PDA first appeared in January 1992, referring to the _____
a) Apple Newton
b) IBM Simon
c) Nokia Communicator
d) Palm TX
e) none of the above

1.1.7.5 The _____ can be considered the first smartphone.
a) Apple Newton
b) IBM Simon
c) Nokia Communicator
d) Palm TX
e) none of the above

1.1.8.1 A _____ is a computer used by a user to connect to a network and make requests
   a) client
   b) server
   c) peer
   d) all of the above
   e) none of the above

1.1.8.1 A _____ is a computer that receives and responds to requests from other machines
   a) client
   b) server
   c) peer
   d) all of the above
   e) none of the above

1.1.8.2 On a _____ network, each host has equivalent responsibilities and status
   a) democratic
   b) host to host
   c) peer to peer
   d) all of the above
   e) none of the above

1.4.3 True-False

1.1.3. One of the reasons that Babbage failed to make a working difference engine is that he turned his attention to a more advanced design which he called the *analytical engine*

1.1.4 By the 1940's it was becoming clear that electronic devices could do computation faster than mechanical devices

1.1.7.3 As of 2018, the fastest supercomputer was the Cray 1

1.1.7.4 Laptop computers have developed to the point that they have essentially the same capabilities as desktop computers.

1.1.7.8 The reduction in size, price and power consumption of computer components has made it possible to install general purpose computers as embedded systems in many devices)

1.2.1 A computer derives its power not from the ability to perform powerful/complex actions, but rather from sheer speed

1.3.4 The term **hacker** was once used to describe a computer expert who used his technical knowledge to overcome a problem. It has come, in the popular culture, to be used to describe someone who uses his technical knowledge to break into computer systems

1.3.4 As of 2011, the majority of active malware threats were worms or Trojans rather than viruses

1.3.5 Since the early 1980's computer crime and computer related crime have increased.

1.3.5 The discipline of computer forensics is frequently used in civil proceedings.

2. Computer Components

Almost all modern computers have pretty much the same design. They all have the same basic components. These basic components are:

Processor

Processor[xxvii]: The component which actually performs the actions/executes the commands that the computer carries out.

Memory: The component where data, information and programs (codes for commands to be executed) are stored.

RAM

Computer memory (Also often referred to as Primary storage, Random Access Memory or RAM[xxviii]) is typically *volatile* (Volatile means that when the computer is turned off, the contents of memory are erased.)

Secondary Storage: Components that store information / data from one session to another. (*Nonvolatile* storage.) Some of the most common types of secondary storage media are:

Hard disk drives[xxix]

A **hard disk drive (HDD)**, **hard disk**, **hard drive** or **fixed disk** is a data storage device used for storing and retrieving digital information using one or more rigid ("hard") rapidly rotating disks (platters) coated with magnetic material.

Hard Disk Drive (Open)

Optical Storage:

Optical storage is data storage on an optically readable medium [xxx](CD or DVD). Data is recorded by making marks in a pattern that can be read back with the aid of light, usually a beam of laser light precisely focused on a spinning disc. Optical storage differs from other data storage techniques that make use of other technologies such as magnetism or semiconductors.

Optical disk

Flash drives

A [xxxi]**USB flash drive**, also known under a variety of other names, is a data storage device that includes flash memory and has an integrated Universal Serial Bus (USB) interface.

SanDisk Cruzer Micro a brand of USB flash drives

USB flash drives are typically removable and rewritable, and physically much smaller than an optical disc.

Input devices:

Input devices are components/devices which allow us to put information/data *into* the computer memory.

The most common input devices are:

Keyboard

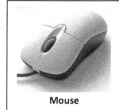

Mouse

^{xxxii}keyboard
^{xxxiii}mouse

Output devices:

Output devices are components/devices which allow the computer to communicate information/data *from* computer memory *to* users and/or other computing devices.

The most common output devices are:

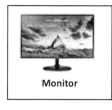

Monitor

Printer

^{xxxiv}monitors
^{xxxv}printers

Communications Devices:

Communications devices are devices which facilitate communication with other devices. These include: Network Interface Controller (**NIC**), Wireless communications devices, Bluetooth interface controllers, Ethernet ports, modems

Bus:

The component which facilitates movement of data from one place to another within the computer.

In most systems, these components will be either mounted on or connected to the computer's ^{xxxvi}*motherboard*.

A *motherboard* (also called a *system* board) is a circuit board.

Electronic components are attached to, or, in some cases, built into, the motherboard.

motherboard

2.1 Central Processing Unit (CPU)

The CPU interprets and carries out the basic instructions that result in the computer doing what we want it to do.

A ^{xxxvii}Central Processing Unit (CPU) has two subdivisions: The *Control Unit* and the *Arithmetic Logic Unit* (ALU)

CPU

The [xxxviii]*Control Unit* directs and coordinates the operations of the computer. It identifies the memory location containing the code for the operation to be carried out, then identifies the operation, then locates any data to be used in the operation, then initiates the action to carry out the operation.

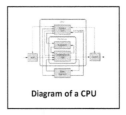

Diagram of a CPU

The *ALU* performs arithmetic operations (addition, subtraction, multiplication, division, comparison) on the data supplied by the control unit

The processor relies on a crystal circuit called the [xxxix]Clock *Generator*. The clock generates electronic pulses (called ticks or clock cycles) at regular intervals. These clock ticks **control** the *timing* of the computer operations.

A desktop PC clock generator

2.1.1 Overclocking

In an effort to get better performance, some users change the system clocks on their computers to run at higher speeds. This is called "overclocking".

Overclocking will result in a system that runs faster but it can cause data errors. The CPU might read the content of a cell before it has stabilized. The most common problem, however, is overheating. If a CPU runs at a higher speed, it will use more energy and produce more heat.

2.2 Memory

The term "memory", (or *primary* memory, or primary storage) refers to *addressable* semiconductor memory, i.e. integrated circuits consisting of silicon-based transistors, resistors capacitors, etc.

Most semiconductor memory consists of binary *memory cells* (flip-flops which can be in one of two states), each storing one *bit* (0 or 1).

Since the information stored in an individual memory cell is so limited, the cells in computer memory are arranged in groups of 8 cells (each group of 8 cells is referred to as a *byte*).

Each byte is assigned a number as its *address*. The address is used to identify the individual byte and to allow the computer to identify the byte and reference its contents or to change its contents.

The *contents* of the memory cells (the collection of 0's and/or 1's that are the states of the memory cells) are used to represent information.

Of course, the content of a single cell can only represent one of two items, 0 representing one of them and 1 representing the other.

In order to deal situations involving more than two values, it is *necessary* to use *groups* of cells. As mentioned above, the most common kind of group is the *byte*, consisting of 8 cells.

27

The time it takes for the processor to reference a memory cell is pretty much independent of where it is located in memory. That is the reason for the term *random access* memory.

This makes it different from other direct-access data storage media (such as hard disks, CD's, DVD's.) For those types of media the time required to read and write data items varies significantly depending on their physical locations on the recording medium.

The time difference is due to mechanical considerations, such as media rotation speeds and arm movement delays.

There are two distinct types of memory: *Random Access Memory* (RAM) and *Read Only Memory* (ROM)

The computer can read information from, but cannot write to, locations in ROM. Most home or office computers include magnetic disk drives and have only a minimal hardware initialization core and bootloader in ROM (known as the BIOS in IBM-compatible computers.) This is the minimum configuration necessary to allow the computer to load the rest of the operating system from disk into RAM. This arrangement results in an operating system that is relatively easy to upgrade.

ROM is implemented using *nonvolatile* types of memory (The contents do not change when the computer is powered down and then later restarted.)

Data items can be read from both RAM and ROM, but can be *written* only to locations in RAM.

RAM is normally associated with *volatile* types of memory. (When the computer *is turned off the contents of volatile memory are erased.)*

Access to locations in RAM is generally much faster than to locations in ROM. This is one of the reasons that only minimal initialization software will be in ROM.

There are, in fact several different types of RAM, some of which are much faster than others (and more expensive and use more power and generate more heat.)

In order to achieve greater execution speed but hold costs down, computer manufacturers use relatively cheap memory for most of their RAM, but include a small amount of (more expensive) high speed circuitry. This is called *cache memory*.

A system will attempt to store in cache memory, information that is likely to be accessed frequently, and/or in the immediate future.

2.3 Secondary Storage:

Secondary storage (also known as external memory or auxiliary storage), differs from primary storage in that it is not directly accessible by the CPU. The computer usually uses its input/output channels to access secondary storage and transfers the desired data using intermediate areas in primary storage (These areas are called *buffers*). Secondary storage does not lose the data when the device is powered down (it is *non-volatile.*) It is also typically two orders of magnitude less expensive than primary storage but access to secondary storage is much slower than primary storage access.

Modern computer systems typically have two orders of magnitude more secondary storage than primary storage.

In modern computers, [xl]hard disk drives are normally used as secondary storage. The time taken to access a given byte of information stored on a hard disk is typically a few thousandths of a second, (a few *milliseconds*.)

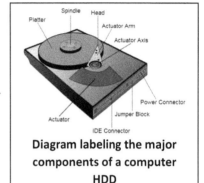

By contrast, the time taken to access a given byte of information stored in random-access memory is measured in billionths of a second (*nanoseconds*.)

Diagram labeling the major components of a computer HDD

This illustrates the significant access-time difference between solid-state memory and rotating magnetic storage devices: hard disks are typically about a million times slower than primary memory.

Rotating *optical storage devices* (such as CD and DVD drives), have even longer access times.

With disk drives, once the disk read/write head reaches the proper placement and the data of interest rotates under it, subsequent data on the same track are relatively fast to access.

To reduce the seek time and rotational latency, data are transferred to and from disks in large contiguous blocks.

2.4 Input Devices:

Clearly, users will need some way to enter information into their computers.

To facilitate this, the computers must be connected to some kinds of *input devices*.

Traditional input devices include the keyboard, mouse and scanner. More recently touch screens and cameras built into smartphones/tablets have also become widely used.

2.4.1 Keyboard:

A [xli]**keyboard** is a typewriter-style device, which uses buttons or keys, to act as mechanical levers or electronic switches.

Keyboard

Many (most) early computers used [xlii]punched cards for their primary input, but by the late 1980's, interaction via keyboard had become the most common input method.

Punched card for a
FORTRAN program

2.4.2 Mouse:

A [xliii]mouse is a pointing device that detects motion on a surface. This motion is typically translated into the motion of a pointer/cursor on a display. This supports interaction with a graphical user interface (*GUI*).

Mouse

The cursor is a symbol on the screen (usually a blinking vertical bar) that indicates where the next user interaction (character entered from keyboard, mouse button clicked) will have its effect.

A mouse will normally have two or more buttons that the user can press (click) to interact with the GUI.

The movements of the mouse on the surface are used to control the position of the pointer on the screen. The pointer identifies the place where actions of the user take place. Hand movements are replicated by the pointer. Clicking or hovering (stopping movement while the cursor is within the bounds of an area) can select files, programs or actions from a list of names, or (in graphical interfaces) through small images called "icons" and other elements.

For example, a text file might be represented by a picture of a paper notebook, and clicking while the cursor hovers over this icon might cause a text editing program to open the file in a window

2.4.3 Scanner:

An [xliv]**image scanner** — (usually just called a **scanner**) is a device that optically scans pictures, print documents, handwriting, or objects, and creates digital images of them.

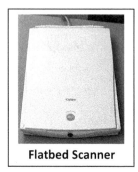

Flatbed Scanner

Variations of the *flatbed scanner* (where the document is placed on a glass window for scanning) are commonly found in offices.

2.4.4 Touchscreen:

A [xlv]touchscreen is a visual display which is sensitive to where a user is pressing on it and transmits this information to the computer.

> Users can give input by touching the screen with their fingers and/or a special stylus/pen.

> Some touchscreens require users to wear specially coated gloves, and others use a special stylus/pen.

A user can use the touchscreen to react to what is displayed and to control how it is displayed (for example by zooming the text size).

Capacitive touchscreen of a mobile phone

A touchscreen enables the user to interact directly with what is displayed, rather than using an intermediate device, such as a mouse, touchpad, etc.

Touchscreens are common in devices such as game consoles, tablet computers, and smartphones.

The popularity of smartphones, tablets, and many types of information appliances is driving an ever-increasing demand for, and acceptance of, touchscreens on portable and functional electronics.

> Touchscreens are also found in the medical field and in heavy industry, as well as for automated teller machines (ATMs), and [xlvi]kiosks

> > Kiosks such as museum displays where keyboard and mouse systems do not allow a suitably intuitive, rapid, or accurate interaction by the user with the display's content.

An Internet kiosk in
Hemer, Germany

2.4.5 Digital Cameras:

Digital cameras store images in a digital format. These images can be stored on portable media (such as a flash drive) and this media can be used to, transfer them to a computer's memory or storage.

In fact, many computers (especially laptops, tablets and smartphones) come with digital cameras built in. This makes it even more convenient to transfer the graphic images (digital photos) into the computer where they can be processed using graphic editing software and/or sent to others using communications software.

2.5 Output Devices

When a computer has finished carrying out its information processing, the user would probably want to know something about what the results were (why else would he/she be using the computer?)

For the computer to communicate the processing results, it needs some kind of *output device*.

> An **output device** is a piece of computer equipment used to communicate the results of data processing that an information processing system (such as a computer) has carried out

An output device converts the electronically generated information into a form that a human-can see, read, hear, feel, ... somehow get a sense of what the results of the processing were.

The most common kinds of output devices can be divided into two classes: those that produce output that users can *see* and those that produce output that users can *hear*.

2.5.1 Audio output devices:

Audio output devices can, in turn, be divided into two classes: those designed to broadcast sound more or less publicly, so that most people within a reasonable area can hear it, and those designed to produce output for only one person.

2.5.1.1 Speakers

Computer [xlvii]speakers are output devices used by the computer to produce sounds.

Computer speakers

Computer Speakers can be built into the motherboard or can be attached as external (peripheral) units.

2.5.1.2 Headphones:

[xlviii]Headphones are low volume speakers that are placed on a band around the user's head, holding them close to, or even in the ears. The speakers produce sounds of volume so low that only the user can hear them. They may be used to prevent other people from hearing the sound either for privacy or to prevent disturbance, as in listening in a public library. They can also provide a level of sound fidelity greater than loudspeakers of similar cost. Part of their ability to do so comes from the lack of any need to perform room correction treatments with headphones.

[xlix]Headphones are also useful for video games, as they allow players to judge the position of an off-screen sound source (such as the footsteps of an opponent or their gun fire).

In-ear headphones

Headphones

2.5.2 Visual Display Devices

There are two general classes of visual display devices: those that produce output in a form referred to as soft copy (devices on which the output is temporary) and those that produce hard copy output (output in physical form.).

2.5.2.1 Screen (Monitor)

The term *monitor* [also referred to as a **video display terminal (VDT)** and **video display unit (VDU)**] refers to a display screen for video images, (and case that holds it.)

Monitors are clearly soft copy devices, since their displays are regularly modified and/or replaced.

The early computer monitors were constructed like the early TVs, as a CRT (Cathode Ray Tube) with a fluorescent screen. Today, monitors are created using *flat panel display technology*.

2.5.2.1.1 [1]Flat panel technology

Flat panel technology encompasses a growing number of electronic visual display technologies. They are far lighter and thinner than traditional CRT television sets and video displays. They are usually less than 10 centimeters (3.9 in.) thick.

Flat Panel Display

Most of the modern flat-panel displays use *LCD* (liquid crystal display) technologies. Some, however, use *plasma display technology*

Most LCD screens are back-lit to make them easier to read in bright environments. They are thin and light and provide good linearity and resolution.

Liquid crystal displays are lightweight, compact, portable and cheap and they are more reliable, and easier on the eyes than are CRTs.

Very large displays frequently use plasma display technology.

2.5.2.1.2 Organic Light-Emitting Diode (OLED)

An **organic light-emitting diode** (**OLED**) is a light-emitting diode (LED) embedded on flexible plastic. They are used to create displays on flexible materials for use in such applications as wearable devices and on curved surfaces and surfaces that change shape.

2.5.2.2 Projectors

A [li]**projector** or **image projector** is a device that projects an image (or moving images) onto a surface, such as a projection screen.

Projector

Earlier projectors created their images by shining a light through lenses, but many newer types of projectors can project the image directly, by using lasers.

The very newest types of projectors are handheld projectors. Current handheld models do not produce very bright images, and their projections are hard to see if there is much ambient light

2.5.2.3 Printers

A [lii]printer is an output device that prints graphics or text on paper or similar physical media.

Printer

Printers produce hard copy output, as opposed to the previously described devices which were all soft copy devices.

The two most common kinds of printer are laser printers and inkjet printers.

Monochrome (black and white) laser printers are commonly found in offices, where they are used to produce text documents. Color laser printers are more expensive than monochrome, but their prices are going down, and they are becoming more common

Inkjet printers are cheaper than laser printers and can produce relatively high quality color output. They are commonly found in homes and small businesses.

2.6 Communications Devices

There are several kinds of communications devices used in computers. Some duplicate the functionalities of others, although in different ways, and some provide relatively specialized services.

2.6.1 NIC's

Many computers come with communications devices preinstalled. The most common of these devices is the *Network Interface Controller* (**NIC**)

> A **network interface controller** is a computer hardware component that connects a computer to a computer network.

> Early network interface controllers were commonly implemented on expansion cards that plugged into a computer bus, but most modern computers have a network interface built into the motherboard.

2.6.2 Wireless

Most modern *laptops* come with hardware capable of communicating wirelessly with a router or with other computers.

> Wireless hardware for a desktop computer eliminates the need to run network cable from the router to the computer.

> Wireless hardware can also give a laptop or desktop computer the capability to communicate wirelessly with other computers, without the need for a router.

2.6.3 Bluetooth

[liii]Bluetooth is a wireless technology now included on many smartphones, laptops and desktop computers. It allows the computer to communicate wirelessly with other devices that have the hardware necessary to send and/or receive Bluetooth signals.

A typical Bluetooth mobile phone headset.

> One popular way of utilizing Bluetooth technology on a computer is with a mouse capable of Bluetooth communication, which eliminates the need for a wire.

Wireless control of and communication between a mobile phone and a handsfree headset was one of the earliest applications to become popular

2.6.4 Ethernet Ports

The[liv] Ethernet port is another popular communication device that comes built into most personal computers. It allows the computer to communicate with another computer, a router or other networking device using Ethernet cable.

Ethernet Port

> Some laptop manufacturers, wanting to offer models that are as light and simple as possible, have opted to remove the Ethernet port and allow users to rely on the laptop's wireless card,

> This might be an indication of the future of personal-computer communications hardware.

35

2.6.5 Modems

A [lv]**modem** (**mo**dulator-**dem**odulator) is a network hardware device that encodes (*modulates*) digital information to be transmitted using carrier wave signals to be transmitted and then decoded (*demodulated*) by another modem at the receiving unit. (Often the carrier waves are audio signals carried by telephone lines but modems can be used with any means of transmitting analog signals. Currently the most common form of modem is the *cable modem* which allows access to high speed Internet service through the cable television network.

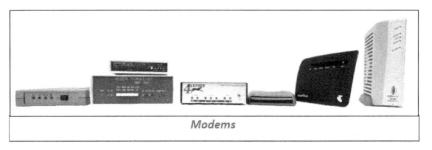

Modems

2.6.5.1 Digital Transmission on Telephone Lines

The first modems made use of telephone connections. They simply transmitted and detected sounds using combinations of frequencies. It was originally thought that it was not possible to operate conventional phone lines beyond about 9600 bit/s. In the late 1980's, however, techniques were developed for extending the bandwidth available on these lines. In particular, *asymmetric digital subscriber loop* (ADSL, or more commonly just DSL) which uses different wave lengths (and different bandwidths) for the uploading and downloading of data.

A DSL connection can be deployed over existing cable. Such deployment, even including equipment, is much cheaper than installing a new, high-bandwidth fiber-optic cable over the same route and distance. The commercial success of DSL and similar technologies largely reflects the advances made in electronics over the decades that have increased performance and reduced costs even while digging trenches in the ground for new cables (copper or fiber optic) remains expensive. Telephone companies were pressured into moving to ADSL largely due to competition from cable companies. Demand for high bandwidth applications, such as video and file sharing, also contributed to popularize ADSL technology

2.7 Bus:

A bus is a physical arrangement that facilitates the transmission of data from one place in the computer to another.

There are various kinds of buses in a computer for different specific functions, that is, for transmitting different specific kinds of information.

Some of them are: data bus; address bus; universal serial bus (USB)

Early computer buses were parallel electrical wires with multiple connections, but the term is now used generally for any arrangement that provides the function of transmitting data.

2.8 Questions:

2.8.1 Completion

2. The component which actually performs the actions/executes the commands that the computer carries out is called the processor or _____

2.1 The _____ interprets and carries out the basic instructions that result in the computer doing what we want it to do

2.2 The term "memory", (*primary* memory, primary storage) is _____ semiconductor memory, i.e. integrated circuits consisting of silicon-based transistors

2.2 Data items can be read from both RAM and ROM, but can be *written* only to locations in _____

2.2 Most home or office computers include magnetic disk drives and have only a minimal hardware initialization core and bootloader in ROM (known as the _____in IBM-compatible computers).

2.2 In order to achieve greater execution speed but hold costs down, computer manufacturers use relatively cheap memory for most of their RAM, but include a small amount of (more expensive) high speed circuitry. This is called _____memory

2.4 Traditional _____devices include the keyboard, mouse and scanner.

2.4.2 A text file might be represented by a picture of a paper notebook, and clicking while the cursor hovers over this _____might cause a text editing program to open the file in a window

2.4.4 A(n) _____is a visual display which is sensitive to where a user is pressing on it and transmits this information to the computer

2.5.2.1.1 Very large displays generally use _____*display technology*

2.5.2.1.2 OLED's are used to produce _____ displays

2.5.2.2 The two most common printer mechanisms are black and white _____ printers, used primarily for common text documents, and color inkjet printers

2.5.2.3 The newest types of projectors are _____projectors

2.6.3 Wireless control of and communication between a mobile phone and a handsfree headset was one of the earliest applications of _____ to become popular

2.8.2 Multiple Choice

2. Computer memory (Primary storage, Random access memory or RAM) is typically _____(when the computer is turned off, the contents of memory are erased.)
   a) short term
   b) volatile
   c) temporary
   d) all of the above
   e) none of the above

2. Almost all modern computers have pretty much the same design. They all have the same basic components. One of these basic components would be:
   a) Processor
   b) Primary storage
   c) Secondary storage
   d) all of the above
   e) none of the above

2. In most systems, the basic components will be mounted on or connected to the computer's _____
   a) motherboard
   b) CPU
   c) bay
   d) bus
   e) none of the above

2.1 The central processing unit has two subdivisions, the control unit and the

_____
a) CPU
b) ALU
c) VDU
d) OSU
e) none of the above

2.2 ROM is implemented using _____ types of memory
a) expensive
b) inexpensive
c) volatile
d) nonvolatile
e) none of the above

2.2 RAM is implemented using _____ types of memory
a) expensive
b) inexpensive
c) volatile
d) nonvolatile
e) none of the above

2.3 On modern computers _____ are normally used for secondary storage
a) hard disk drives
b) optical drives
c) flash drives
d) all of the above
e) none of the above

2.3 The time taken to access a given byte of information stored on a hard disk is typically a few thousandths of a second, (a few_____.)
a) microseconds
b) milliseconds
c) nanoseconds
d) macroseconds
e) none of the above

2.3 The time taken to access a given byte of information stored in random-access memory is measured in billionths of a second (_____.)
a) microseconds
b) milliseconds
c) nanoseconds
d) macroseconds
e) none of the above

2.4.3 Variations of the _____*scanner* (where the document is placed on a glass window for scanning) are commonly found in offices
  a) flatbed
  b) business
  c) digital
  d) all of the above
  e) none of the above

2.5.2.1.1 Most of the modern flat-panel displays use _____ technologies
  a) CRT
  b) LCD
  c) VDT
  d) DVD
  e) none of the above

2.5.2.1.1 Liquid crystal displays are _____
  a) cheaper and more reliable than CRT's
  b) cheaper but less reliable than CRT's
  c) More reliable but more expensive than CRT's
  d) more expensive and less reliable than CRT's
  e) none of the above)

2.6.4 An Ethernet port is an example of a(n) _____ device
  a) input
  b) output
  c) communications
  d) storage
  e) none of the above

2.7 A USB is a type of:
  a) bus
  b) motherboard
  c) data storage device
  d) input device
  e) none of the above

2.8.3 True-False

2. Almost all modern computers have pretty much the same design. They all have the same basic components

2.2 The time it takes for a program to execute depends very much on where it is located in computer memory, since it takes the processor much longer to reference some cells than others.

2.2 Access to locations in RAM is generally much faster than to locations in ROM

2.3 Secondary storage does not lose the data when the device is powered down (it is *non-volatile*.) It is also typically two orders of magnitude more expensive than primary storage.

2.3 Rotating *optical storage devices* (such as CD and DVD drives), have much shorter access times than do rotating magnetic storage devices, such as hard disks.

2.4.4 Very few tablet computers incorporate touchscreens, since their larger screens would make them too expensive.

2.4.5 Most laptops and tablets come with digital cameras built in.

2.5.2. Headphones cannot provide good quality sound. For good fidelity, speakers are needed.

2.6.1 Early network interface controllers were commonly built into computer motherboards, but most on most modern computers, they are implemented on expansion cards that plugged into a computer bus.

3 Software

Of course a computer is of little use if it does not have programs to execute, programs that will make it do what the user wants it to do. Computer programs (collectively known as *Computer Software*) can generally be divided into two classifications: ***System Software*** and ***Application Software***

System software is software which provides an interface and services both for users and for other software.

Application software is software designed to provide specific services for users.

3.1 System Software

System software is often divided into two classifications: **Operating Systems** (often referred to as simply *OS*'s) and **Utility Programs**

3.1.1 Operating Systems

The *operating system* (prominent current examples include UNIX, Microsoft Windows, Mac OS X, Android, iOS, and Linux), allows the components of a computer to work together.

An operating system would include programs that interface:

- users with hardware;
- users with software;
- software with hardware;
- software with other software.

An operating system will perform tasks like transferring data between memory and disks and like rendering output onto a display device.

3.1.1.1 Single Tasking Systems

The earliest operating systems required users to type their programs (and their operating system commands) on punched cards. The cards would be placed (in proper order) into a card reader. The cards would be read and the program executed. These operating systems were inherently single tasking systems, executing one program at a time, finishing one program before beginning the next.

3.1.1.2 Multi-Tasking Systems

In the early days of computing, CPU time was expensive, and peripherals were very slow. When the computer ran a program that needed access to a peripheral, the central processing unit (CPU) would have to stop executing program instructions while the peripheral processed the data. This was usually very inefficient.

The first computer using a multitasking system was the British *Leo III* owned by J. Lyons and Co. (First completed in 1961.) During batch processing, several different programs would be loaded in the computer memory, and the first one would begin to run. When the first program came to an instruction that required waiting for response from a peripheral, the context of this program was stored away, and another program in memory was given a chance to run. This process of running until required to wait, and, passing control to another program, rather than stopping and waiting, would continue until all programs finished running

3.1.1.3 Multi User Systems / Time Sharing Systems

With computers loading several programs into memory at once, (Multitasking systems) it seemed natural to allow several users to interact with the system concurrently (Multi-User systems)

Instead of submitting programs as a sequence of punched cards, the user would interact with the system by means of a "monitor" (in the early days this was often an [lvi]ASR 33 teletype)

In order to better support multi user systems the concept of "time slicing" was developed. The CPU would be assigned to execute commands from one process for a short period of time (slice), then from another process for a period (slice) of time, … (The idea being that each user would have the impression that the computer was continually working for him.)

A Teletype Model 33 ASR teleprinter, with punched tape reader and punch, usable as a computer terminal

3.1.1.3.1 Dartmouth Time Sharing System (DTSS)

The first successful multiuser time sharing system was at Dartmouth College. It began operations on May 1, 1964. and remained in operation until the end of 1999. Its implementation began in 1963, by a student team under the direction of John Kemeny and Thomas Kurtz and had the aim of providing easy access to computing facilities for all members of the college. Kemeny felt that 10 seconds was the maximum time that a user should have to wait for a system response[3]. The system provided interactive time-sharing for up to nearly 300 simultaneous users in the 1970s (a very large number at that time.)

---

[3] 10 seconds might seem quite a long wait time today, but users of the single user systems common at that time would typically have to wait overnight, and a waiting times of several days was not uncommon.

3.1.1.3.2 UNIX

Probably the most widely used multi-user operating system now is UNIX, developed by Thompson and Ritchie at AT&T's Bell Labs in 1969.

Although UNIX was originally only intended just for use inside the Bell system, its use soon spread widely first to academic institutions and shortly thereafter to vendors such as IBM, SUN microsystems and Microsoft, under proprietary names such as XENIX (Microsoft) AIX (IBM) and SOLARIS (SUN)

UNIX spread so widely in part because it was designed to be easily portable to a wide range of different computing systems. It was developed as a collection of individual modules (utilities) and written in a high level language (C) which made it easy to modify and keep up to date.

3.1.1.4 Personal Computer Operating Systems

A **personal computer** is a multi-purpose electronic computer whose size, capabilities, and price make it feasible for individual use. Personal computers are intended to be operated directly by an end-user who is not necessarily a computer expert or technician.

The computer time-sharing models that were typically used with larger, more expensive minicomputer and mainframe systems, were not appropriate for the earliest personal computers.

Personal computers DO, however, require some kind of operating system to allow their users to execute programs, store files, and, in general USE their computers.

The earliest personal computers generally featured operating systems with rather primitive command line interfaces.

3.1.1.4.1 Command Line Interface

The command line system was more or less inherited from the earlier multi user systems.

In a system with a command line interface, the user would use the keyboard to enter a computer command. The computer would interpret the command and execute it. Then the computer would wait for the user to enter another command.

Some of the more widely used operating systems with command line interfaces were: AppleDOS, CP/M and MS-DOS.

3.1.1.4.2 Graphical User Interfaces (GUI's)

In the early 1980's an alternative means for users to communicate with and control their personal computers began to emerge.

The **graphical user interface (GUI)**, is a type of user interface that allows users to interact with electronic devices through graphical icons and visual indicators, instead of text-based user interfaces. GUIs were introduced in reaction to the perceived steep learning curve of command-line interfaces

Alan Kay used a GUI as the main interface for the Xerox Alto computer, released in 1973. Most modern general-purpose GUIs are derived from this system, although it never reached commercial production.

The first commercially available computer with a GUI was the 1979 PERQ workstation, manufactured by Three Rivers Computer Corporation.

In 1981, Xerox eventually commercialized the Alto in the form of a new and enhanced system – the Xerox 8010 Information System – more commonly known as the Xerox Star.

These early systems spurred many other GUI efforts, including the Apple Lisa in 1983, the Apple Macintosh 128K in 1984, and the Atari ST with Digital Research's GEM, and Commodore Amiga in 1985. Of these, the Apple Macintosh was probably the most influential.

The Xerox Star 8010 workstation introduced the first commercial GUI.

3.1.1.4.2.1 Mac OS

The [lvii]"classic" Mac OS is the original Macintosh operating system that was introduced in 1984 along with the first Macintosh computer and it remained in primary use on Macs through 2001. It was originally named "System Software", or simply "System"; Apple rebranded it as "Mac OS" in 1996.

The original Macintosh System Software and Finder, released in 1984

Mac OS is characterized by its monolithic system. It was noted as being easy to use, but was criticized for its limited memory management, lack of memory protection and access controls, and for its propensity for conflicts among extensions.

3.1.1.4.2.2 Microsoft Windows

Microsoft introduced an operating environment named *Windows 1.0* on November 20, 1985, as a graphical operating system shell for MS-DOS in response to the growing interest in graphical user interfaces (GUIs). Windows 1.0 was intended to compete with Apple's operating system, but achieved little success.

Windows 2.0 was released in December 1987, and was more popular than its predecessor. It resulted in Apple Computer filing a suit against Microsoft alleging infringement on Apple's copyrights. (eventually settled in court in Microsoft's favor in 1993)

[lviii]Windows 3.0, released in 1990 is the first Microsoft Windows version to achieve broad commercial success.

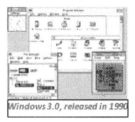
Windows 3.0, released in 1990

Microsoft Windows came to dominate the world's personal computer (PC) market with over 90% market share.

On PCs, Windows is still the most popular operating system. However, in 2014, Microsoft admitted losing the majority of the overall operating system market to Android, because of the massive growth in sales of Android smartphones. In 2014, the number of Windows devices sold was less than 25% that of Android devices sold. Of course the two operating systems are for very different platforms.

3.1.1.4.2.3 Linux Systems

Linux is an open source computer operating system derived from UNIX, first released on September 17, 1991 by Linus Torvalds.

Linux was originally developed for Intel x86 based personal computers, but has since been ported to more platforms than any other operating system.

Because of the dominance of Android (a version of Linux) on smartphones, Linux has the largest installed base of all general-purpose operating systems.

Linux is also the leading operating system on servers and other big iron systems such as mainframe computers, and is used on 99.6% of the TOP500 supercomputers.

It is used by around 2.3% of desktop computers. The Chromebook, which runs on Chrome OS (another Linux derivative), dominates the US K–12 education market and represents nearly 20% of the sub-$300 notebook sales in the US.

Desktop Linux distributions include a windowing system, and an accompanying desktop environment such as [lix]GNOME or KDE.

GNOME 2.0, June 2002

KDE 3.2 with Konqueror and the About screen

3.1.1.5 Smart Phones

A **smartphone** is a mobile phone with a built in computer and operating system that normally combines features of a personal computer operating system with other features useful for mobile or handheld use.

Smartphones are generally about pocket-sized and typically have the features of a mobile phone (they can make and receive voice calls and they can send and receive text messages.) They also have the features of other mobile devices/utilities,

Features such as event calendars; media players; video games; GPS navigation; digital cameras; and video cameras.

Smartphones can access the Internet and can run a variety of third-party software components.

These components are called "apps" and can be obtained from places like Google Play Store or Apple App Store.

A smartphone typically has a color display with a graphical user interface that covers more than 75% of the front surface. The display is almost always a touchscreen, and sometimes also has a touch-enabled keyboard. The user can press onscreen icons to activate "app" features, or he/she can use the virtual keyboard to type words and numbers.

The vast majority of modern smartphones use one of two operating systems: Android or iOS

3.1.1.5.1 Android

[lx]**Android** is a mobile operating system developed by Android Inc. (starting in 2003) (later purchased by Google in 2005.) It is based on Linux and is designed primarily for touchscreen mobile devices such as smartphones and tablets.

Android works with a user interface that is principally based on direct manipulation. It uses touch gestures that loosely correspond to real-world actions, such as swiping, tapping and pinching These are used to manipulate on-screen objects (icons)

Nexus 7 tablet, running Android 4.1 Jelly Bean

Android typically includes a virtual keyboard for text input. In addition to touchscreen devices, Google has further expanded the system to include Android TV for televisions, Android Auto for cars, and Android Wear for wrist watches, each with a specialized user interface.

Variants of Android are also used on notebooks, game consoles, digital cameras, and other electronics.

In September 2015, Android had 1.4 billion monthly active users, and it has the largest installed base of any operating system.

3.1.1.5.2 iOS

[lxi]**iOS** is a mobile operating system created and developed by Apple Inc. exclusively for its hardware. It is the operating system that presently powers many of the company's mobile devices, including the iPhone, iPad, and iPod Touch. It is the second most popular mobile operating system globally after Android. iPad tablets are also the second most popular, by sales (second to Android) since 2013.

The iOS user interface is based on direct manipulation, using multi-touch gestures. It implements interface control elements including *sliders*, *switches*, and *buttons*. Interaction with the

iOS on Smartphone

system includes *gestures* such as *swipe*, *tap*, *pinch*, and *reverse pinch*, all of which have specific definitions within the context of the iOS operating system and its multi-touch interface. Internal accelerometers are used by some applications to respond to shaking the device or rotating it.

3.1.1.5 Smart TV's

Since smart TV's include computing systems, they need operating systems to make them functional. As in a personal computer, a TV OS will have a graphical user interfaces (GUI) to support user interaction.

TV operating systems allow a user to browse not just channels on satellite or cable TV but also on demand video services. The systems also access pictures, music or video content on connected storage devices.

There is no standard operating system or interface for smart TVs. Some of the more widely used are: Roku TV, Android TV, FireTV, WebOS, Tizen, Smartcast and MyHomeScreen.

3.1.2 Utility Programs

Utility programs help system administrators analyze, configure, optimize and maintain the computer. They include programs for things like virus protection, access control, file system administration, display control, system restore and backup, and system security. The term *system software* can also be used for software development tools (like compilers, linkers and debuggers)

3.1.3 Device Drivers

As computers became more and more common, manufacturers began producing devices and equipment to work with the computers (printers, modems, scanners, projectors, disk drives, …) Of course, the different companies did not produce equipment that worked in exactly the same way, and of course the computer manufacturers (and software designers) could hardly be expected to know all of the details of how every one of the different kinds of equipment would operate, so the equipment manufacturers began designing "drivers" to go with their equipment.

A device driver is a computer program that operates or controls a particular kind of device that might be attached to a computer. A driver provides an interface for a device. Drivers enable operating systems, and other computer programs, to access functions without needing to know precise details of the hardware.

When a device is installed on a computer, its drivers must also be installed. For early personal computer users, the process of installing drivers was often difficult and frustrating. As microprocessors made mass-market computers affordable, personal computers became more common and an automated system for driver installation and configuration became more and more important.

Early systems for software configuration of devices included the MSX standard, NuBus, Amiga Autoconfig, and IBM Microchannel. Initially all expansion cards for the IBM PC required configuration by physical selection on the board with jumper straps or DIP switches, but increasingly ISA bus devices were arranged for software configuration. By 1995, Microsoft Windows included a comprehensive method of enumerating hardware at boot time and allocating resources. The system was called the "Plug and Play" standard.

Now, there are several completely automated computer interfaces, none of which requires any device configuration by the computer user. The only task of the user is to load software. The devices are self-configuring.

3.2 Application Software

An *application* is any program, (or group of programs), that is designed to be used by regular users (end users) as opposed to systems administrators. Application software (also called *end-user programs*) includes such things as database programs, word processors, Web browsers and spreadsheets.

The collective noun **application software** refers to all *applications* collectively. This distinguishes it from *system* software, which is mainly involved with running the computer.

Applications may be bundled with the computer and its system software or published separately, and may be coded as proprietary, open-source or university projects. Apps built for mobile platforms are called *mobile apps*.

There are many types of application software:

- An *application suite* (or software suite) consists of multiple applications bundled together. They usually have related functions, features and similar user interfaces. They are often able to interact with each other, e.g. open each other's files.

    o Business applications often come in suites, e.g. Microsoft Office, LibreOffice and iWork, which bundle together a word processor, a spreadsheet, etc.; but suites exist for other purposes, e.g. graphics or music.

- *Enterprise software* addresses the needs of an entire organization's processes and data flows, across several departments, often in a large distributed environment.

    o Examples include enterprise resource planning systems, customer relationship management (CRM) systems and supply chain management software.

    o Departmental Software is a sub-type of enterprise software with a focus on smaller organizations or groups within a large organization. (Examples include travel expense management and IT Helpdesk.)

- *Enterprise infrastructure software* provides common capabilities needed to support enterprise software systems. (Examples include databases, email servers, and systems for managing networks and security.)

- *Information worker software* lets users create and manage information, often for individual projects within a department, in contrast to enterprise management.

- o Examples include time management, resource management, analytical, collaborative and documentation tools.

- o Word processors, spreadsheets, email and blog clients, personal information system, and individual media editors may aid in multiple information worker tasks.

- *Content access software* is used primarily to access content without editing, but may include software that allows for content editing. Such software addresses the needs of individuals and groups to consume digital entertainment and published digital content.

  - o Examples include media players, web browsers, and help browsers.

- *Educational software* is related to content access software, but has the content or features adapted for use in by educators or students.

  - o For example, it may deliver evaluations (tests), track progress through material, or include collaborative capabilities.

- *Simulation software* simulates physical or abstract systems for either research, training or entertainment purposes.

- *Media development software* generates print and electronic media for others to consume, most often in a commercial or educational setting. This includes graphic-art software, desktop publishing software, multimedia development software, HTML editors, digital-animation editors, digital audio and video composition, and many others.

- *Product engineering software* is used in developing hardware and software products. This includes computer-aided design (CAD), computer-aided engineering (CAE), computer language editing and compiling tools, integrated development environments, and application programmer interfaces.

- *Entertainment Software* can refer to video games, screen savers, programs to display motion pictures or play recorded music, and other forms of entertainment which can be experienced through use of a computing device.

3.2.1 Productivity Software

Productivity software is a term that has come to be used to describe a type of software that helps users produce things. In particular software that helps in the production of business related things such as documents, databases, graphs, worksheets and presentations.

Common examples of office productivity software include word processors, database management systems (DBMS), graphics software and spreadsheet applications. The term is sometimes also used for any type of application that is used to help people do their jobs, and is used for programs supporting collaboration and communication.

3.2.2   Classes of Software

The way software is marketed/distributed can be categorized in several different ways. Among the classifications are: commercial software, shareware, freeware, public domain software and software as a service (SaaS).

> (These classes are not entirely mutually exclusive, and there is some dispute as to the exact definitions of the terms.)

Most software is covered by copyright which provides legal basis for owners to establish their rights.

3.2.2.1 Commercial software

Software that you buy. Proprietary software vendors can prohibit users from sharing the software with others. Another unique license is required for another party to use the software. A software vendor spells out the specific terms of use in an <u>end-user license agreement</u> (EULA). The user may agree to this contract in writing, interactively on screen, or just by opening the box containing the software. License agreements are usually not negotiable, but vendors will sometimes grant rights to the user in the license agreement. Vendors typically limit the number of computers on which software can be used, and prohibit the user from installing the software on extra computers, except in the case of the purchase of the right to do so (site license.).

3.2.2.2 Shareware

During the 1980's several independent software authors, lacking financial means to mount large scale advertising campaigns, developed a new system for marketing their products. They distributed free copies of their programs, recommended that people who received the programs copy them and give the copies to friends, family, colleagues and/or anybody who might have an interest. It was suggested (but not required) that, if, after using the programs for a period of time, the user wanted to continue using them, they might send some kind of payment to the program authors.

3.2.2.3 Freeware

Freeware is software that is available for use at no monetary cost. In other words, while freeware may be used without payment it is most often proprietary software, and usually modification, re-distribution or reverse-engineering without the author's permission is prohibited. Two historic examples of freeware include Skype and Adobe Acrobat Reader. Freeware, although itself free of charge, may be intended to benefit its producer. The source code of freeware is typically not available.

3.2.2.4 Open Source Software

Open-source software (OSS) is a type of computer software whose source code is released under a license in which the copyright holder grants users the rights to study, change, and distribute the software to anyone and for any purpose. Open-source software is often developed in a collaborative public manner.

3.2.2.5 SaaS

Software as a service (or SaaS) is a way of delivering access to centrally hosted applications over the Internet—as a service. SaaS applications are sometimes called web-based software, on-demand software, or hosted software. Whatever the name, SaaS applications run on a SaaS provider's servers. Instead of installing and maintaining software, you simply access it via the Internet, freeing yourself from complex software and hardware management. The provider manages access to the application, including security, availability, and performance. SaaS business applications are usually accessed by users using a web browser. Unlike traditional software, which is conventionally sold as a perpetual license with an up-front cost (and an optional ongoing support fee), SaaS providers generally price applications using a subscription fee, most commonly a monthly fee or an annual fee.[1]

SaaS has become a common delivery model for many business applications.

Centralized hosting of business applications dates back to the 1960s. Starting in that decade, IBM and other mainframe providers conducted a service bureau business, often referred to as time-sharing or utility computing. Such services included offering computing power and database storage to banks and other large organizations from their worldwide data centers. As businesses and individuals began to acquire their own computers, this type of service became less widely used until the expansion of the Internet during the 1990s brought about a new class of centralized computing, called Application Service Providers (ASP). ASPs provided businesses with the service of hosting and managing specialized business applications, with the goal of reducing costs through central administration and through the solution provider's specialization in a particular business application.

Software as a Service essentially extends the idea of the ASP model. However:

- While most initial ASP's focused on managing and hosting third-party software, as of 2012 SaaS vendors typically develop and manage their own software.
- Whereas many initial ASPs offered more traditional client-server applications, which require installation of software on users' personal computers, SaaS solutions of today rely predominantly on the Web and only require a web browser to use.

3.3 Ethical Issues Related to Computer Software

Ethical issues related to computer software can be divided into two categories:

- issues related to users of computers and their software
- and issues for software developers (and distributers)

3.3.1 Ethical Issues for Software Users

3.3.1.1 Piracy

The following is copied from
http://cs.stanford.edu/people/eroberts/cs201/projects/software-piracy/ethical.html

The Ethics of Piracy

The software pirates and those trying to protect software copyrights approach the ethics of piracy from two different viewpoints. There are two contrasting ethical views on the issue of piracy, and both have their valid points.

Piracy is Ethical

Some think that there is nothing wrong with software piracy. They believe in the freedom of information and expression (ie. "information wants to be free"). According to them, it is acceptable and ethical to copy the software because they have a right to the information contained in the software. They also hold the idea of that reproduction and distribution of software a part of fair use within copyright law.

Some pirates have cited their first amendment rights as an excuse for piracy. They claim that since posting information in electronic form is protected by the first amendment, the distribution of illegal software is an exercise of the rights of self-expression and should not be infringed upon.

Some think that software piracy doesn't hurt anyone, that it is a victimless crime. They believe that, with the rising prices of software, software manufacturers are really not hurt by pirates making illegal copies of their programs. They think since they are not going to pay for the software anyway, it is OK to get it free.

Another common excuse runs along the lines of "the software is really not worth the money they're charging anyway." The argument continues that since the software is buggy, it's really not a crime to distribute faulty products.

Finally, some claim that they're simply "testing" the software. "If I really like it, I'll pay for it," runs the common excuse, "but this program just sits on my hard drive and I almost never use it."

Piracy is Unethical

This view holds that piracy is really not a victimless crime. Due to software piracy, the industry has seen some 12 billion dollars and over 100,000 jobs lost. The attraction of piracy is due to its anonymity and the ease with which illegal copies of software can be made and distributed. However, every person who makes illegal copies is contributing to the monetary losses caused by piracy.

Information really does not "want to be free." People who write the software have rights to profit from it, just as people who write books have the sole right to sell them. Copying software is depriving the rightful owners of software of hard-earned wages.

Software piracy cannot be protected by the first amendment, because the first amendment does not cover illegal activities. Just as yelling "Fire!" in a crowded theater is not protected by the first amendment, neither is the distribution of illegal software.

The claim that pirates have a right to make illegal copies of software because the software is buggy, or too expensive, or not frequently used by the pirate, is also flawed. Someone might think a Rolls-Royce is too expensive and not worth the money, but this doesn't give him the right to steal it. Or, the fact that you almost never watch television doesn't give you the right to steal a TV.

Pirating software costs everyone. Since not as many copies of software are sold, the software manufacturers have to raise prices. This means that the legitimate users are incurring higher costs due to piracy.

In short, piracy is not as "victimless" a crime as it may seem. Software developers, distributors, and, ultimately, end users, are all hurt by piracy.

3.3.1.2 Ethical and Unethical Uses of Computers and Computer Programs

The widespread use of computers has introduced a new level of insecurity into all of our lives, and provided most of us with new opportunities to engage in new behaviors, many of which have the potential of being unethical

3.3.1.2.1 Unethical Behavior

The computers in our lives give us the opportunity to engage in new activities, many of which are at best questionable, and many of which are clearly unethical. Among these activities are software piracy, cyberbullying, plagiarism, unauthorized access to private information spreading of viruses, and monitoring the computer activities of others.

Given the widespread use of computers (and especially smartphones) by children, the situation has evolved to where parents now have responsibilities (for which they are for the most part woefully unprepared) to prevent their children from engaging in unethical behaviors.

3.3.1.2.1.1 Piracy

The issue of software piracy is dealt with at great length in another section, but there is no question that accepting unauthorized copies of software, and/or allowing friends and associates to make copies of software you have purchased would be illegal, in addition to being, at the very best, questionable, ethically speaking.

3.3.1.2.1.2 Cyberbullying

Although bullying has always been a part of life, the emergence of social networking has given enormously greater powers to would be bullies. (A number of widely publicized incidents in which the victims were driven to suicide can attest to this.)

Clearly the parents of would be victims have a responsibility to protect their children from these online predators, but the parents of potential bullies also have a moral/ethical responsibility to monitor their children, and to prevent them from engaging in such behavior.

3.3.1.2.1.3 Plagiarism

Documents with all kinds of information are widely available on the Internet (as well as images and videos) and software to copy from the online documents and paste what was copied into documents of our own is also generally available. It is easy to forget our ethical (and legal) duty to attribute the source of what we are using.

There is also a booming cottage industry of people who will write papers and do homework assignments for high school and college students. Needless to say, submitting someone else's work as one's own is frowned on by teachers everywhere, and must be considered an ethical violation.

3.3.1.2.1.4 Unauthorized access

Computer ethics also involve avoiding unauthorized access to computer systems and preserving the confidentiality and privacy of data in computers. In addition, it gives us all the responsibility of respecting system policies, such as not sharing passwords and not trying to access unauthorized sites.

This becomes somewhat controversial in the case of a parent accessing the memory and browser history of their child's computer or smartphone. How old does the child have to be before it becomes improper for the parent to do this?

3.3.1.2.1.5 Spreading viruses

Since we know that harmful viruses exist, if we share software and/or data with others, we have an ethical responsibility to make sure that what we share is virus free.

3.3.1.2.1.6 Activity monitoring

In the area of the ethics of activity monitoring, there are many questions, but few clear answers.

Some employers make it a practice to monitor employees' activities while at work, even to the point of recording all of their email accesses. Many people argue that this is an invasion of privacy. Others argue that the employer is paying for the employees' time, and, usually, for the computers they are using and for the Internet access, as well. One might argue, then. That this would give the employer the right to ensure that the employees are using the computers (and Internet access) for work related activities.

Whichever argument you believe, it would seem clear that *secret* monitoring of *anybody's* activities would be ethically wrong.

Or would it be? Don't police do that regularly when investigating suspected lawbreakers? Is it ethically permissible for police to do it? Under what circumstances? Should they be required to obtain a warrant?

Parents have not only a right, but a responsibility to monitor the activities of their children, or at least the activities of *young* children. At some point the parents no longer have such rights or responsibilities. At what age does this change take place?

3.3.1.2.2 Insecurities

The simple fact that we have and use a computer puts us at risk of a number of possible dangers, any or all of which can and should worry us.

3.3.1.2.2.1 Identity Theft

One of the things we must be aware of is the possibility of identity theft.

Identity theft is the deliberate use of someone else's identity. The person whose identity has been assumed may suffer adverse consequences if they are held responsible for the perpetrator's actions. Identity theft occurs when someone uses another's identifying information, (like their name, ID number, credit card number), without their permission, usually to commit fraud or other crimes.

The majority of identity theft victims do not realize that they are victims until their lives have been negatively impacted. Many people do not find out that their identities have been stolen until they are contacted by financial institutions or discover suspicious activities on their bank accounts. According to an article by Herb Weisbaum, everyone in the US should assume that their personal information has been compromised at some point. It is therefore of great importance to watch out for warning signs that your identity has been compromised.

3.3.1.2.2.2 Cyberbullying

A frequently used definition of cyberbullying is "an aggressive, intentional act or behavior that is carried out by a group or an individual, using electronic forms of contact, repeatedly and over time against a victim who cannot easily defend him or herself."

There are many variations of this definition, such as the National Crime Prevention Council's more specific: "the process of using the Internet, cell phones or other devices to send or post text or images intended to hurt or embarrass another person."

> Components such as the repetition of the behavior and the power imbalance between the bully and victim, and their applicability to electronic harassment, are debated.

Cyberbullying is often similar to traditional bullying, although there are some distinctions. Victims of cyberbullying may not know the identity of their bully, or why the bully is targeting them. The harassment can have wider-reaching effects on the victim than traditional bullying, as the content used to harass the victim can be spread and shared easily among many people, and often remains accessible for a long time after the initial incident. The victim is also sometimes exposed to the harassment whenever they use technology, as opposed to traditional harassment where the bully often must be in physical proximity to the target.

3.3.1.2.2.3 Being Hacked

Many people get hacked and do not even have a clue about it, till it is too late. If you do not want to have your computer hacked, you really have to be on alert and remain vigilant for strange behavior in e-mail messages, credit card statements and unusual computer behavior.

3.3.1.2.2.4 Infection by Viruses

Computer viruses currently cause billions of dollars' worth of economic damage each year. The damage is due to system failure, waste of computer resources, data corruption, increased maintenance costs, etc. In response, an industry of antivirus software has cropped up, selling or freely distributing virus protection to users of various operating systems.

No currently existing antivirus software is able to detect all computer viruses (especially new ones), but computer security researchers are actively searching for new ways to enable antivirus solutions to more effectively detect emerging viruses, before they have already become widely distributed.

3.3.1.2.2.5 Being Monitored by Employers

The following is copied from:
https://www.privacyrights.org/consumer-guides/workplace-privacy-and-employee-monitoring#

Technology allows employers to monitor many aspects of their employees' workplace activities. While employees may feel that such monitoring is a violation of their privacy rights, many types of monitoring are allowed under the law. A majority of employers monitor their employees. They are motivated by concern over litigation and the increasing role that electronic evidence plays in lawsuits and government agency investigations.

Employers use technology to provide insight into employee behavior based on the trail of "digital footprints" created each day in the workplace. This technology can piece together all of these electronic records to provide behavior patterns that employers may utilize to evaluate employee performance and conduct. For example, it might look for word patterns, changes in language or style, and communication patterns between individuals. This makes it possible for employers to monitor many aspects of their employees' jobs, especially on telephones, computer terminals, through email and voice mail, and when employees are online.

Almost everything you do on your office computer can be monitored. Such monitoring is virtually unregulated. Therefore, unless company policy specifically states otherwise (and even this is not assured), your employer may listen, watch and read most of your workplace communications. Courts often have found that when employees are using an employer's equipment, their expectation of privacy is limited.

It's important to be aware that your employer's promises regarding workplace privacy issues may not always legally binding. Policies can be communicated in various ways: through employee handbooks, via memos, and in union contracts. For example, if an employer explicitly states that employees will be notified when telephone monitoring takes place, the employer generally must honor that policy. There are usually exceptions for investigations of wrong-doing. If you are not already aware of your employer's workplace privacy policies, it is a good idea to become informed.

3.3.1.3 10 Commandments of Computer Ethics

Written by the Computer Ethics Institute

1. Thou shalt not use a computer to harm other people.
2. Thou shalt not interfere with other people's computer work.
3. Thou shalt not snoop around in other people's computer files.
4. Thou shalt not use a computer to steal.
5. Thou shalt not use a computer to bear false witness.
6. Thou shalt not copy or use proprietary software for which you have not paid.
7. Thou shalt not use other people's computer resources without authorization or proper compensation.
8. Thou shalt not appropriate other people's intellectual output.
9. Thou shalt think about the social consequences of the program you are writing or the system you are designing.
10. Thou shalt always use a computer in ways that ensure consideration and respect for your fellow humans.

3.3.2 Ethical Issues for Software Producers

There is software designed specifically to monitor computer activity (keyboard logging software is one common type.). Families and business people often use *keyloggers* to monitor network usage, frequently without their users' direct knowledge. Many of these programs seem to be marketed to individuals looking for evidence that a spouse might be cheating. Surely *suspicion* of infidelity should not be sufficient grounds for making such violation of privacy acceptable behavior. One must ask, then, how ethical is the behavior of the *marketers* of such software?

Software developers (and software vendors) are required to make decisions with moral and ethical consequences on a daily basis.

The following is a thoughtful analysis, copied from:
http://www.infoworld.com/article/2607452/application-development/12-ethical-dilemmas-gnawing-at-developers-today.html

What follows are a few of the ethical quandaries confronting developers every day - - whether they know it or not. There are no easy answers, in some measure because the very nature of the work is so abstract. To make matters worse, business has become so inextricably linked with computer technology that it is difficult to balance the needs and motivations of all invested parties in trying to prevent today's business-case feature from becoming tomorrow's Orwellian nightmare.

The trick is to think past the current zeitgeist and anticipate every future utilization of what you build. Pretty simple, huh? Consider this less of a guidebook for making your decisions and more of a starting point for the kind of ethical contemplation we should be doing as a daily part of our jobs.

3.3.2.1 Ethical dilemma No.1: Log files--what to save and how to handle them

Programmers are like pack rats. They keep records of everything, often because it's the only way to debug a system. But log files also track everything users do, and in the wrong hands, they can expose facts users want kept secret.

Many businesses are built on actively protecting log files. Some remote-backup services even promise to keep additional copies in disparate geographic locations. Not every business aspires to such diligence. Snapchat, for example, built its brand on doing a very bad job of backing up data, but its users are attracted by the freedom of the forgetful system.

The mere existence of log files begs several ethical questions. Are they adequately protected? Who has access? When we say we destroy the files, are they truly destroyed?

The crux is ascertaining what information is worth keeping, given the risks of doing so, ethical or otherwise. Here, the future complicates the equation. In the 1960s, smoking was widely embraced. No one would have thought twice about keeping track of people's smoking habits. Today, however, the knowledge of someone's smoking activity can be used to raise health insurance rates or even deny coverage.

Future business deals; future government regulations; an unforeseen, desperate need for new revenue streams -- it may be impossible to predict what seemingly innocent log file will become problematic in the future, but it is essential to consider the ethics of how you handle the logs along the way.

3.3.2.2 Ethical dilemma No.2: Whether-and how-to transform users into products

It's a well-worn adage of the startup era: If you're not paying for a service, you're not a customer; you're the product.

On the Internet, "free" services abound. In fact, the question of where the money will come from is often put off, being off putting. We just build the amazingness, keep an eye on the adoption metrics, and figure someone else will take care of the dirty work of keeping the server lights on. Worst case, there are always ads.

Developers need to be upfront about who will support their work and where the money will come from. Any changes should be communicated to users in a clear, timely fashion to avoid shock and blowback. Transforming people into products is an ethical shift not to be taken lightly. Shady ad deals, shady ad networks -- we need to be careful how we handle the implicit trust of early adopters.

3.3.2.3 Ethical dilemma No.3: How free does content really want to be?

A number of businesses depend on serving up content without paying those who create it. Some turn around and sell ads or even charge for access. These businesses often couldn't survive and couldn't price their material as attractively if they had to shoulder their fair share of the development costs. They develop elaborate rationalizations about "sharing" or "fair use" to cover up an ethically shaky decision.

Developers must ask themselves how their code will support everyone in the food chain, from creators to consumers. Do the people creating the content want their work to be distributed this way? Are they happy to work for exposure or attention alone? Are they given a fair share of the revenue?

Not considering these questions amounts to turning a blind eye to piracy. After all, not all information just "wants to be free."

3.3.2.4 Ethical dilemma No.4: How much protection is enough

Some say that everything should be double-encrypted[4] with two different algorithms and locked in a hard disk that is kept in a safe. Alas, the overhead slows

---

[4] **Encryption** is the process of encoding a message or information in such a way that only authorized parties can access it and those who are not authorized cannot. Encryption does not itself prevent interference, but denies the intelligible content to a would-be interceptor. Computer Security Institute reported that in 2007, 71% of companies surveyed utilized encryption for some of their data in transit, and 53% utilized encryption for some of their data in storage. Most modern encryption systems are *public key* systems. In public-key encryption schemes, the

the system to a crawl and makes development 10 times more onerous. To make matters worse, if one bit gets flipped or one part of the algorithm is wrong, the data is all lost because the encryption can't be undone.

Others don't want to lift a finger to protect the data. The next team can add special encryption later if it's necessary, the developers might say. Or they might argue that there's nothing sensitive about it. Teams that ignore these responsibilities are usually able to generate plenty of other code and create piles of wonderful features that people crave. Who cares if they're secure?

There's no simple answer to how much protection to apply. There are only guesses. More is always better -- until the data is lost or the product doesn't ship.

3.3.2.5   Ethical dilemma No.5: To bug-fix or not to bug-fix?

It's hard enough to negotiate the ethical shoals when they involve active decisions, but it's even harder when the problem can be pushed aside and labeled a bug that will be fixed eventually. How hard should we work to fix the problems that somehow slipped into running code? Do we drop everything? How do we decide whether a bug is serious enough to be fixed?

Isaac Asimov confronted this issue long ago when he wrote his laws of robotics and inserted one that forbid a robot from doing nothing if a human would be harmed through the robot's inaction. Of course his robots had positronic brains that could see all the facets of a problem instantly and solve them. The questions for developers are so complicated that many bugs go ignored and unfixed because no one wants to even think about them.

Can a company prioritize the list fairly? Are some customers more important than others? Can a programmer play favorites by choosing one bug over another? This is even more difficult to contemplate when you realize that it's hard to anticipate how much harm will come from any given bug.

3.3.2.6   Ethical dilemma No. 6: How much to code -- or compromise -- to prevent misuse

The original Apple Web camera came with a clever mechanical extra, a physical shutter that blocked the lens when it was off. The shutter and the switch were linked together; there was no way to use the camera without opening the shutter yourself.

Some of the newer webcams come with an LED that's supposed to be illuminated when the camera is activated. It usually works, but anyone who has programmed a

---

encryption key is published for anyone to use and encrypt messages, but only the receiving party has access to the decryption key that enables messages to be read. Public-key encryption was first described in a classified document in 1973.Before then all encryption schemes were symmetric-key (also called private-key). A publicly available public key encryption application called Pretty Good Privacy (PGP) was written in 1991 by Phil Zimmermann, and distributed free of charge with source code;

computer knows there may be a place in the code where the camera and the LED can be decoupled. If that can be found, the camera can be turned into a spying device.

The challenge for the engineer is anticipating misuse and designing to prevent it. The Apple shutter is one of the obvious and effective examples of how it can be done elegantly. When I was working on a book about cheating on the SAT, I met one hacker who was adding networking software to his calculator. After some deliberation, he decided to only support wired protocols because he was afraid kids would sneak a calculator with Wi-Fi into an exam. By supporting only wired protocols, he ensured that anyone in a test would need to run a wire to their neighbor's machine. He hated skipping the wireless protocols, but he felt the risk of abuse was too high.

3.3.2.7 Ethical dilemma No.7: How far to defend customers against data requests

If you collect data, it's a safe bet that your organization will someday be caught between serving your customers and serving the government. Requests to deliver data to legal entities are becoming increasingly common, leaving more and more software and services organizations to contemplate to what extent they will betray their customers' privacy before the law. You can scrutinize these requests and even hire your own lawyers to contest whether they are truly lawful, but the reality is that the courts will be debating legalities long after your funding runs out.

There are no easy solutions. Some companies are choosing to leave the business rather than lie to their customers. Others are trying to be more open about requests, which the government often tries to forbid.

3.3.2.8 Ethical dilemma No.8: How to deal with the international nature of the Internet

The Internet runs everywhere, avoiding many of the traditional barriers at the borders. This can be a recipe for legal headaches when customers A and B are in different countries. That's only the beginning, because servers C and D are often in entirely different countries as well.

This leads to obvious ethical issues. Europe, for instance, has strict laws about retaining personal information and views privacy breaches as ethical failures. Other countries insist on companies keeping copious records on dealings. Whose laws should a company follow when customers are in different countries? When data is in different counties? When data is transferred across international lines?

Keeping up with every legal contingency can be Herculean, leaving many organizations surely tempted to bury their heads in the sand.

3.3.2.9 Ethical dilemma No.9: How much to give back to open source

Everyone knows that open source is free. You don't pay anything and that's what makes it so wonderful and complex. But not everyone contemplates the ethical issues that come with using that free code. All of the open source packages come with licenses and you need to follow them.

Some of the licenses don't require much sacrifice. Licenses like the Apache License or the MIT License require acknowledgement and that's about it. But other licenses, such as the GNU General Public License, ask you to share all your enhancements.

Parsing open sources licenses can present ethical challenges. One manager from a big public company told me, "We don't distribute MySQL, so we don't owe anyone anything." He was keying on the clause, written decades ago, that tied the license's obligations to the act of redistributing software. The company used MySQL for its Web apps, so he felt it could take without giving back.

There are no simple ways to measure the ethical obligations, and many programmers have wasted many keystrokes arguing about what they mean. Still, the entire endeavor will grind to a halt if people stop giving. The good news is that it's often in everyone's best interest to contribute because everyone wants the software to remain compatible with their use of it.

3.3.2.10 Ethical dilemma No.10: How much monitoring is really warranted

Maybe your boss wants to make sure the customers aren't ripping off the company. Maybe you want to make sure you get paid for your work. Maybe some spooky guy from the government says you must install a backdoor to catch bad guys. In every case, the argument is filled with assurances that the backdoor will only be used, like Superman's powers, to support truth and justice. It won't be used against political enemies or the less fortunate. It won't be sold to despotic regimes.

But what if the bad guys discover the hidden door and figure out how to use it themselves? What if your backdoor is used to support untruths and injustices? Your code can't make ethical decisions on its own. That's your job.

3.3.2.11 Ethical dilemma No. 1: How bulletproof should code really be

Sure, the minimal calculation, simple data structure, and brute-force approach works well in demo when the problems are small. The users try out the code and say, "Gosh this works quickly." Several months later, when enough data has been loaded into the system, the cheap algorithm's weaknesses appear and the code slows to a crawl. Developers must often decide exactly how hard to work on the final product. Do you whip off a quick and cheap solution or spend weeks adding bulletproof code that deals with extreme cases? True, clients and users should assume some of the responsibility during the requirements and sign-off phases, but developers are often better equipped to anticipate potential contextual hiccups of running code.

3.3.2.12 Ethical dilemma No.12: How much should future consequences influence present decisions

Many projects don't make waves. The information goes in and never escapes. Some, however, take on a life of their own, escaping into the wild where they may do untold harm. Security, penetration testing, espionage -- these are obvious candidates for considering the collateral damage of your code.

Take Stuxnet, a virus widely considered a tool for attacking the centrifuges used to purify uranium in Iran. Perhaps it succeeded, but now it lives on, floating along in Windows systems throughout the world.

For most developers, the collateral damage is less obvious. We code for today -- a hard enough proposition -- but we should also consider the future.

Some programmers, for example, love to write complex code that integrates with the operating system and installs new or more complicated drivers. Is that going to work in the future? Will it play well with other new drivers? Will it work with the next generation of the OS? Or will your software leave people with a computer that runs slower and fails more frequently even when your software isn't running?

It may seem simple, but choosing whether to stick with the APIs or follow the standards is an ethical decision. Yes, technology is evolving quickly, and a slavish devotion to outdated mandates can be a hindrance to progress. But we need to consider our part in writing code that lasts a bit longer and not take the decision to swim outside our lane lightly. We can always ask for changes to the standards or the APIs if we need them.

3.4 Questions

3.4.1 Completion

3. _____ software is software which provides an interface and services both for users and for other software

3. _____ software is software designed to provide specific services for users.

3.1.1.4.2.2 On PCs, _____ is the most popular operating system

3.1.1.4.2.3 _____ has been ported to more platforms than any other operating system

3.1.1.4.2.3 _____ has the largest installed base of all general-purpose operating systems

3.1.1.5.2 In the iOS operating system, internal _____ are used by some applications to respond to shaking the device or rotating it

3.1.2 The term *system software* can also be used for software development tools (like_____, linkers and debuggers)

3.2 _____software (also called *end-user programs*) includes such things as database programs, word processors, Web browsers and spreadsheets

3.2 The collective noun **application software** refers to all *applications* collectively. This distinguishes it from _____ software, which is mainly involved with running the computer.

3.2 An *application* _____ consists of multiple applications bundled together. They usually have related functions, features and similar user interfaces. They are often able to interact with each other, e.g. open each other's files

3.2 _____*Software* can refer to video games, screen savers, programs to display motion pictures or play recorded music

3.3.1.1 Some pirates have cited their _____amendment rights as an excuse for piracy

3.4.2 Multiple Choice

3. Computer programs (collectively known as *Computer Software*) can generally be divided into two classifications:
   a) System Software and User Software
   b) System Software and Application Software
   c) Network Software and User Software
   d) Network Software and Application Software
   e) none of the above

3. _____ software is software which provides an interface and services to users and other software
   a) System
   b) User
   c) Network
   d) Application
   e) none of the above

3. _____ software is software designed to provide specific services for users
   a) System
   b) User
   c) Network
   d) Application
   e) none of the above

3.1.1.2 The first computer using a multitasking system was the_____
   a) IBM 360
   b) Colossus Mark I
   c) LEO III
   d) ENIAC
   e) none of the above

3.1.1.3.1 The first successful multiuser time sharing system was
a) DTSS
b) UNIX
c) Multics
d) ENIAC
e) none of the above

3.1.1.3.2 Probably the most widely used multi-user operating system is
a) DTSS
b) UNIX
c) Multics
d) ENIAC
e) none of the above

3.1.1.4.1 _____ is a personal computer operating system with a command line interface.
a) AppleDOS
b) CP/M
c) MS-DOS
d) all of the above
e) none of the above

3.1.1.4.2 _____ is a type of user interface that allows users to interact with electronic devices through graphical icons and visual indicators, instead of text-based user interfaces
a) CLI
b) GVI
c) GUI
d) all of the above
e) none of the above

3.1.1.5.1 Android works with a user interface that is mainly based on direct manipulation, using touch gestures that loosely correspond to real-world actions, such as_____, to manipulate on-screen objects
a) swiping
b) tapping
c) pinching
d) all of the above
e) none of the above

3.2 Business applications often come in_____, e.g. Microsoft Office, LibreOffice and iWork, which bundle together a word processor, a spreadsheet, etc
a) combos
b) suites
c) factions
d) all of the above
e) none of the above

3.4.3 True-False

3.1.1.2 In the early days of computing, CPU time was expensive, and peripherals were very slow.

3.1.1.4 The earliest personal computers generally featured operating systems with rather primitive command line interfaces.

3.1.1.4 Personal computers are intended to be operated directly by an end-user who is not necessarily a computer expert or technician.

3.1.1.4.2 The first commercially available computer with a GUI was the Apple Macintosh.

3.1.1.5 The vast majority of modern smartphones use one of three operating systems: Android, Linux, or iOS.

3.2 A *Web Browser* is considered to be a systems program.

3.3.1.1 There are two contrasting ethical views on the issue of piracy, and both have their valid points.

3.3.1.2.1.6 Some employers make it a practice to monitor employees' activities while at work.

3.3.1.2.2.1 The majority of identity theft victims do not realize that they are victims until it has negatively impacted their lives.

3.3.1.2.2.2 Traditional bullying is much more serious than cyberbullying.

3.3.1.2.2.4 Computer viruses currently cause hundreds of thousands of dollars worth of economic damage each year.

4   [lxii]System Unit

In a desktop computer, most of the electronic components are housed in an enclosure a called the [lxiii]*system unit*. These units are usually rectangular, most are made of steel, aluminum and/or plastic. Most of them used to be painted gray, but recently other colors have become more common.

System Unit

[lxiv]4.1   Motherboards

A **motherboard** (also known as the *mainboard* or *system board*) is the main printed circuit board (PCB) found in general purpose microcomputers and other expandable systems.

It holds the electronic components of a system, such as the *central processing unit* (CPU) and *memory*, and allows communication between many of them. It also provides connectors for other peripherals.

Motherboard

The term *Motherboard* specifically refers to a PCB with expansion capability. It will typically have components attached to it. These often include peripherals, interface cards, sound cards, video cards, network cards, hard drives, and/or other forms of persistent storage; and a variety of other custom components.

4.1.1   [lxv]CPU: Microprocessor

A **central processing unit** (**CPU**) is electronic circuitry within a computer that carries out the instructions of a computer program by performing the basic arithmetic, logical, control and input/output (I/O) operations specified by the instructions.

Microprocessor

Principal components of a CPU include the arithmetic logic unit (ALU) that performs arithmetic and logic operations, processor registers that supply operands to the ALU and store the results of ALU operations, and a control unit that orchestrates the fetching (from memory) and execution of instructions by directing the coordinated operations of the ALU, registers and other components.

Most modern CPUs are microprocessors, meaning they are contained on a single integrated circuit (IC) chip.

4.1.1.1   Processor Size

Modern microprocessors are often described as being 8 bit, 16 bit, 32 bit or 64 bit processors. This description is somewhat ambiguous, since it can refer to (and has been used to refer to) either the number of lines in the data bus (how many bits can be transferred simultaneously) or the number of bits in the address bus (describing the potential amount of memory for the computer) or the number of bits in one of the processor's registers (how many bits can be processed simultaneously) At the moment, most personal computers have 64 bit processors (in all senses of the term.)

Some microprocessors are described as being *dual core* or *quad core* (and probably higher number core by now.) These processors have essentially two or four (or more) processing units built into a single CPU chip, allowing the computer to process data faster by doing several things at the same time.

4.1.1.2 Processor Speed

There are several common measures of how fast processors operate:

Hertz (or megahertz or gigahertz.) This describes the *clock* speed of the processor

This gives a rough (and not very accurate) description of how fast the processor processes data. It is not a very accurate measure of how fast a processor operates because different operations require different numbers of clock pulses, so different programs (using different instructions) will yield different results.

MIPS (**M**illion **I**nstructions **P**er **S**econd) which actually describes how fast the processor executes *instructions*

This measure is more accurate, but can also be misleading, again, because some instructions take longer than others.

FLOPs (**FLO**ating point **O**perations **P**er second, usually seen as gigaflops) Most commonly used describing high performance computing, or sometimes in gaming systems.

4.1.1.3 Classes of Processors

There are two classes of processors – RISC and CISC

Reduced Instruction Set Computing (RISC) is a CPU design strategy based on the insight that a simplified instruction set can provide higher performance. The simplified instruction set allows the CPU to be optimized to execute these instructions more efficiently.

Complex Instruction Set Computing (CISC) is a CPU design strategy based on the idea that with a larger, more complex instruction set, programs can be written using fewer instructions, and thus run faster.

4.2 Memory

Memory (aka *primary storage, main memory*) refers to the computer hardware used to store information for immediate use in a computer.

The term "memory", (in the above sense), is often associated with addressable semiconductor memory.

Most semiconductor memory consists of memory cells or bistable flip-flops, each storing one bit (0 or 1)[5]. The memory cells are grouped into *words* of fixed word length, for example 8, 16, 32, 64 or 128 bits. Each *word* is assigned a number as its **address**. A word, and it contents, can be accessed by means of that address. In many systems, *bytes* (8 bit collections) are used as addressable units, with the term word being reserved for other sizes.

4.2.1 RAM

Random access memory (**RAM**[lxvi]) is the best-known form of computer memory. RAM is considered "random access" because you can access any word in memory directly without accessing the previous words first. Some authors refer to this as "direct access" since any word can be referenced "*directly*".

RAM

(Nobody calls it DAM though. Everybody calls it RAM)

4.2.1.1 Addresses

Each word (or byte) in computer memory has a unique *address*, a number which is used in identifying the word/byte whose content is to be read or modified. The address has a binary representation of N, bits, making it possible to store 2^N words in the memory (where N is determined by the CPU and the address bus of the motherboard. Values of 32 and 64 are common in more recent microcomputers),

4.3 Instruction and Machine Cycles

An **instruction cycle** (sometimes called a **fetch–decode–execute cycle**) is the basic process of computer function. It is the process by which a computer retrieves a program instruction from its memory, determines what actions the instruction dictates, and carries out those actions. This cycle is repeated continuously by a computer's central processing unit (CPU), from boot-up to power down

Different CPU's can have different cycles based on different instruction sets, but they will all be generally similar to the following:

Fetch the instruction: The instruction code is retrieved from the memory address that is currently stored in a program counter (PC), and copied into an instruction register (IR). At the end of the fetch operation, the PC will be updated to contain the address of the next instruction that will be read at the next cycle.

---

[5] There is currently a great deal of interest in quantum computing, which functions somewhat differently than described in this section. Whereas common digital computing requires that the data be encoded into binary digits (bits), each of which is always in one of two definite states (0 or 1), quantum computation uses quantum bits or qubits, which can be in superpositions of states. Large-scale quantum computers would theoretically be able to solve certain problems much more quickly than any classical computers. They would, for example, potentially be able to break many of the cryptographic systems in use today.

Decode the instruction: The instruction whose code is in the IR (instruction register) is identified..

Obtain necessary data: In case the instruction requires data stored in memory, the address of that data is computed and the data is copied from memory into *register(s)* in the CPU.

Execute the instruction (Based on the type of instruction the Program Counter may be updated to a different address from which the next instruction will be fetched.)

Store any resulting values

The cycle is then repeated.

4.4 Cache

Cache memory is random access memory (RAM) that a computer microprocessor can access more quickly than it can access regular RAM. This memory can be integrated directly with the CPU chip or placed on a separate chip that has a separate bus interconnect with the CPU. Cache memory is fast but expensive. Traditionally, it is categorized in "*levels*" that describe its *closeness* and accessibility to the microprocessor:

Level 1 (L1) cache is extremely fast but relatively small, and is usually embedded in the processor chip (CPU).

Level 2 (L2) cache is often bigger than L1; it may be located on the CPU or on a separate chip or coprocessor but with a high-speed alternative bus connecting the cache to the CPU, so as not to be slowed by traffic on the main system bus.

Level 3 (L3) cache is typically specialized memory that works to improve the performance of L1 and L2. It can be significantly slower than L1 or L2, but is usually twice the speed of regular RAM. In the case of multicore processors, each core may have its own dedicated L1 and L2 cache, but share a common L3 cache. When an instruction is referenced in the L3 cache, it is typically elevated to a higher tier cache.

4.5 ROM and other Types of Memory

There are two distinct types of memory: *Random Access Memory* (RAM) and *Read Only Memory* (ROM)

Data items can be read from both RAM and ROM, but can only be *written* to locations in RAM.

ROM is implemented using *nonvolatile* types of memory (The contents do not change when the computer is powered down and then later restarted.) RAM, on the other hand, is normally associated with *volatile* types of memory. (When the computer *is turned off the contents of volatile memory are erased.)*

Most home or office computers include magnetic disk drives and have only a minimal program in ROM (known as the BIOS in IBM-compatible computers) which will load the operating system from the disk into RAM when the computer is started.

The operating system runs from RAM rather than ROM because instructions in the operating system are executed very frequently and ROM access is slower than RAM access

This arrangement also allows an operating system to be upgraded relatively easily.

There are, in fact several different types of RAM, some of which are much faster than others (and more expensive and use more power and generate more heat.) These are the kinds of RAM used for cache memory.

4.5.1 CMOS

[lxvii]CMOS (complementary metal-oxide-semiconductor) is a type of integrated circuit that requires very little power, It can store data and execute simple instructions (keeping track of time passing, system time and date, etc) without draining a battery providing the power it needs to operate.

CMOS Battery

CMOS has been used on motherboards to store the BIOS instructions. For this function, it is being replaced by the technology used for SSD-flash drives.

4.6 Data Representation

The primary function of a computer is *information processing*. (This INCLUDES numerical computation, but also involves much more.)

In order for a computer to be able to process information, the information must be represented in a form that the computer can deal with.

For many reasons, computer designers have come to use binary (two state) equipment to store representations of data.

Among the reasons are the following:

Binary devices are relatively cheap to manufacture

Distinguishing between two states is less error prone than distinguishing between more than two states.

The use of binary equipment requires that information be represented in binary form, as sequences of 0's and 1's. Unfortunately, although binary representations are convenient for digital equipment, they are problematic for humans. It is difficult for humans to distinguish between two sequences of binary digits (even recognizing whether they have the same number of digits can be problematic) and this can lead to errors when dealing with information in binary format. To ameliorate this problem it has become common to represent data using a system of 16 digits (a hexadecimal system.) These digits are identified as 0, 1, 2, 3, 4, 5, 6, 7, 8, 9, A. B, C, D, E, and F[6].

These digits represent the binary sequences:

0	-	0000
1	-	0001
2	-	0010
3	-	0011
4	-	0100
5	-	0101
6	-	0110
7	-	0111
8	-	1000
9	-	1001
A	-	1010
B	-	1011
C	-	1100
D	-	1101
E	-	1110
F	-	1111

Thus the binary sequence 1011000100000101 could be represented as B105 and the sequence 1001000010101001 would be represented as 90A9.

4.6.1 Character Codes

We expect our computers to process text data, and so it is necessary that representations of characters (letters, digits, punctuation symbols, etc.) must be stored in computer memory.

4.6.1.1 ASCII

One of the earliest (and still one of the most commonly used) systems for doing this is ASCII (American Standard Code for Information Interchange.)

ASCII is a character encoding standard. ASCII codes are used to represent text in computers, telecommunications equipment, and other devices.

Originally based on the English alphabet, ASCII encodes 128 specified characters into seven-bit integers. The characters encoded are digits *0* to *9* (represented by the codes 48-57), lowercase letters *a* to *z* (represented by the codes 97-122), uppercase letters *A* to *Z* (represented by codes 65-92), basic punctuation symbols, the space symbol and several control codes that originated with Teletype machines.

---

[6]   It is also common to use the lowercase letters a, b, c, d, e and f

Since the ASCII codes use 7 bits, each character can be (and almost always is) represented as content of an 8 bit byte

The extra bit is sometimes used to extend the ASCII system to represent more symbols/characters, but not in a uniformly accepted way. It is more often used for error checking.

4.6.1.2 Unicode

Many languages use symbols/characters that are not included in the ASCII coding system.

The Unicode system was developed in an effort to allow speakers of these languages access to computers.

Unicode is a computing industry standard for the consistent encoding, representation, and handling of text expressed in most of the world's writing systems.

The latest version of Unicode contains a repertoire of more than 128,000 characters covering 135 modern and historic scripts, as well as multiple symbol sets.

4.6.1.3 EBCDIC

IBM had difficulty adjusting their many card punch machines to accommodate ASCII coding, and so developed their own coding system which they called *extended binary coded decimal interchange code* (EBCDIC) which was more compatible with their existing hardware. EBCDIC is an eight-bit character encoding, and was created to extend the existing Binary-Coded Decimal (BCD) Interchange Code, or BCDIC.

EBCDIC was announced with the release of the IBM System 360. When the system 360 became wildly successful, so did EBCDIC. Now all IBM mainframe and midrange peripherals and operating systems use EBCDIC as their inherent encoding

4.7 Adapter cards:

An **adapter card** (expansion card, expansion board, or accessory card) is a printed circuit board that can be inserted into an electrical connector, or expansion slot on a computer motherboard to add functionality to a computer system via the *expansion bus*.

4.7.1 Expansion bus:

An *expansion bus* is a *computer bus* which moves information between the internal hardware components of a computer system (including the CPU and RAM) and peripheral devices. It is a collection of wires and *protocols* that allows for the *expansion* of a computer

4.8 Bay:

A system unit will normally have open spaces built in where equipment such as disk drives can be installed.

These open spaces are called bays, or often drive bays.

A drive bay is a standard-sized area where hardware can be added to a computer.

Over the years since the introduction of the IBM PC, it and its compatibles have had many form factors of drive bays. Four form factors are in common use today, the 5.25", 3.5", 2.5" or 1.8" drive bays. These names do not refer to the width of the bay itself, but rather to the sizes of the disks used by the drives mounted in these bays

Drive bays are most commonly used for the installation of disk drives, although they can also be used for front-end USB ports, I/O bays, card readers, fans, fan controllers, RAID controllers, tool storage, and many other things.

4.9 Connectors and Ports

[lxviii]In computer hardware, a **port** serves as an interface between the computer and other devices.

In computer terms, a port usually refers to the female part of connection.

Computer ports have many applications. They can be used to connect computers to monitors, webcams, speakers, and other peripheral devices

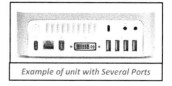
Example of unit with Several Ports

Physically, a computer port is a specialized outlet on a piece of equipment to which a plug or cable connects.

Electronically, the several conductors where the port and cable contacts connect, provide a method to transfer signals between devices

4.9.1 USB Ports

A **USB port** is a standard connection interface for personal computers and consumer electronics devices.

 USB stands for Universal Serial Bus, an industry standard for short-distance digital data communications.

 USB ports allow USB devices to be connected to each other with and to transfer digital data over USB cables.

They can also supply electric power across the cable to devices that need it.

4.9.2 Additional Ports

Electronically, hardware ports can almost always be divided into two groups, based on the way they transfer signals:

> Serial ports and parallel ports

Serial ports send and receive one bit at a time via a single wire pair.

Parallel ports use several sets of wires to transmit multiple bits at the same time.

4.10 Video Connectors

Modern multimedia applications (especially video applications) place greater computational requirements on computing systems than can be met by the normal CPU's (at least without serious degradation of performance in other areas.) As a consequence, most personal computers incorporate specialized video processing units, frequently as adapter cards. These "video cards" include specialized processors (GPU's) to deal with the specialized computations involved in controlling the images to be displayed, and dedicated memory cells specifically for tracking the color and intensity to be displayed at each pixel on the computer output device.

Video output has become so intensive that it requires its own specialized types of transmission cables and connector design.

Digital Video connectors are used to deliver the highest quality video signal.

The technology transmits large amounts of digital data from the source to the display, resulting in a high-quality image.

> DVI (Digital Visual Interface) was developed by the industry body DDWG (the Data Display Working Group) to send digital information from a computer to a digital display, such as a flat-panel LCD monitor.

> HDMI took a step forward by integrating audio and video into a more compact interface.

> DisplayPort is an interface technology that is designed to connect high-graphics capable PCs and displays as well as home theater equipment and displays. DisplayPort is like HDMI in that the DisplayPort signal carries both digital audio and video.

HDMI

DisplayPort

4.11 Questions

4.11.1 Completion

4. In a desktop computer, most of the electronic components are housed in an enclosure a called the _____ unit

4.1 A(n) _____ is the main printed circuit board (PCB) found in general purpose microcomputers and other expandable systems

4.1.1 Most modern CPUs are _____ meaning they are contained on a single integrated circuit (IC) chip.

4.2 Each word in computer memory has a unique_____, a number which is used in identifying the cell to read or modify its contents

4..4 _____ memory, is random access memory (RAM) that a computer microprocessor can access more quickly than it can access regular RAM

4.5.1 _____ is the term usually used to describe the small amount of memory on a computer motherboard that stores the BIOS settings. Some of these BIOS settings include the system time and date as well as hardware settings

4.6.1.16 One of the earliest (and still one of the most commonly used) systems for storing representations of characters in computer memory is_____

4.6.1.2 _____ is a computing industry standard for the consistent encoding, representation, and handling of text expressed in most of the world's writing systems

4.7.1 An *expansion bus* is a *computer bus* which moves information between the internal hardware of a computer system (including the CPU and RAM) and peripheral devices. It is a collection of wires and _____ that allows for the *expansion* of a computer

4.8 A system unit will normally have open spaces built in where equipment such as disk drives can be installed. These open spaces are called _____

4.9 In computer hardware, a(n) _____ serves as an interface between the computer and other computers or peripheral devices.

4.9.1 A **USB port** is a standard cable connection interface for personal computers and consumer electronics devices. USB stands for Universal Serial_____, an industry standard for short-distance digital data communications

4.11.2 Multiple Choice

4 In a desktop computer, most of the electronic components are housed in an enclosure a called the _____.
a) motherboard
b) cache
c) system unit
d) all of the above
e) none of the above

4.1 A _____ is the main printed circuit board found in general purpose microcomputers and other expandable systems.
a) motherboard
b) mainboard
c) system board
d) any of the above
e) none of the above

4.1 The term *Motherboard* specifically refers to a(n) _____ with expansion capability
a) PCB
b) CPU
c) ALU
d) RAM
e) none of the above

4.1.1 A(n) _____ is the electronic circuitry within a computer that carries out the instructions of a computer program by performing the basic arithmetic, logical, control and input/output (I/O) operations specified by the instructions.
a) PCB
b) CPU
c) ALU
d) RAM
e) none of the above

4.1.1.2 One might describe the speed of a microprocessor as a number of _____
a) Hertz
b) MIPS
c) FLOPS
d) any of the above
e) none of the above

4.1.1.3 _____ is a CPU design strategy based on the idea that with a larger, more complex instruction set, programs can be written using fewer instructions, and thus run faster.
a) FLOPS
b) ROM
c) RISC
d) CISC
e) none of the above

4.1.1.3 _____is a CPU design strategy based on the insight that a simplified instruction set can provide higher performance. The simplified instruction set allows the CPU to be optimized to execute these instructions more efficiently
a) FLOPS
b) ROM
c) RISC
d) CISC
e) none of the above

4.2.1.1 Each cell in computer memory has a unique _____, a number which is used in identifying the cell to read or modify its contents
a) ID
b) address
c) locater
d) site
e) none of the above

4.3 An **instruction cycle** (sometimes called a **fetch–decode–execute cycle**) is the basic operational process of a computer. It is the process by which a computer retrieves a program instruction from its memory, determines what actions the instruction dictates, and carries out those actions. This cycle is repeated continuously by a computer's _____, from boot-up to when the computer is shut down.
a) ALU
b) Ports
c) motherboard
d) CPU
e) none of the above

4.4 Cache memory is _____
a) fast but expensive
b) fast and cheap
c) slow and expensive
d) slow and cheap
e) none of the above

4.5 The computer_____, locations in ROM
    a) cannot read information from, and cannot write to
    b) cannot read information from, but can write to
    c) can read information from, but cannot write to
    d) can read information from, and can write to
    e) none of the above

4.5.1 _____ is the term usually used to describe the small amount of memory on a computer motherboard that stores the BIOS settings. Some of these BIOS settings include the system time and date as well as hardware settings.
    a) Cache
    b) CMOS
    c) ASCII
    d) HDMI
    e) none of the above

4.6 The primary function of a computer is _____ *processing.*
    a) information
    b) numerical
    c) binary
    d) ASCII
    e) none of the above

4.7 An _____ is a printed circuit board that can be inserted into an electrical connector, or expansion slot on a computer motherboard to add functionality to a computer system via the *expansion bus.*
    a) adapter card
    b) expansion card
    c) accessory card
    d) any of the above
    e) none of the above

4.8 Drive bays are most commonly used to store _____, ,
    a) disk drives
    b) front-end USB ports
    c) I/O bays
    d) all of the above
    e) none of the above

4.10 _____ is a type of Digital Video connector
    a) DVI
    b) HDMI
    c) DisplayPort
    d) all of the above
    e) none of the above

4.11.3 True-False

4.2.1 RAM is considered "random access" because it is hard to predict how long it will take for the processor to access any given cell.

4.5 ROM access is slower than RAM access

4.5 ROM is implemented using *nonvolatile* types of memory

4.6 Computer designers have come to use analog equipment to store representations of data

4.6.1.1 ASCII codes use 8 bits

4.8 Four form factors are in common use today, the 5.25", 3.5", 2.5" or 1.8" drive bays. These names refer to the width of the disks used by the drives mounted in these bays

5. Input

In computing, an **input device** is a peripheral (piece of computer hardware equipment) used to produce/provide data and control signals for transfer *into* a computer.

Examples of input devices include keyboards, mice, touchscreens, touchpads, scanners, digital cameras and joysticks.

5.1 Keyboards

In computing, a [lxix]**computer keyboard** is a typewriter-style device which uses an arrangement of buttons or keys to act as electronic switches.

Keyboard

A keyboard typically has characters engraved or printed on the keys and each press of a key typically corresponds to a single written symbol.

While most keyboard keys produce letters, numbers or signs (characters), other keys or simultaneous key presses can produce actions or execute computer commands.

Despite the development of alternative input devices, such as the mouse, touchscreen, pen devices, character recognition and voice recognition, the keyboard remains the most commonly used device for direct (human) input of alphanumeric data into computers.

In normal usage, the keyboard is used as a text entry interface to type text and numbers into a word processor, text editor or other programs.

Earlier keyboards had keypress interpretation built in, but in a modern computer, the interpretation of key presses is generally left to the software.

A computer keyboard distinguishes each physical key from every other and reports all key presses to the controlling software.

Keyboards are also used for computer gaming, either with regular keyboards or by using keyboards with special gaming features.

A keyboard can also be used to give commands to the operating system of a computer,

such as Windows' *Control-Alt-Delete* combination, which brings up a task window or shuts down the machine.

Before the development of GUI's (graphical user interfaces) users communicated with their computers' operating systems by typing commands with their keyboards. The commands would be interpreted and executed by a *command line interface*

A command-line interface is a type of user interface operated entirely through a keyboard, or another device doing the job of a keyboard.

5.1.1 Keyboard Types

Computer keyboards differ in size and key spacing, as well as in their form and display.

5.1.1.1 Standard Computer Keyboard

Standard alphanumeric keyboards have keys that are about three-quarters of an inch square, and can be depressed 0.15 to 0.2 inches.

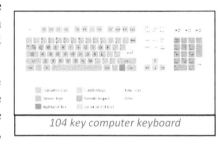

104 key computer keyboard

Desktop computer keyboards, such as the 101-key US traditional keyboards or the [lxx]104-key Windows keyboards, include alphabetic characters, punctuation symbols, numbers and a variety of function keys.

Computer keyboards are similar to electric-typewriter keyboards but contain additional keys, such as the command or Windows keys.

There is no standard computer keyboard, although many manufacturers imitate the keyboard of PCs. There are actually three different PC keyboards: the original PC keyboard with 84 keys, the AT keyboard also with 84 keys and the enhanced keyboard with 101 keys.

The three differ somewhat in the placement of function keys, the control keys, the return key, and the shift key.

5.1.1.2 Laptop Size Keyboards

Keyboards on laptops and notebook computers usually have a shorter travel distance for the keystroke, shorter over travel distance, and a reduced set of keys. They may not have a numerical keypad, and the function keys may be placed in locations that differ from their placement on a standard, full-sized keyboard.

5.1.1.3 Flexible Keyboards

Flexible keyboards combine some characteristics of normal type and laptop type keyboards:

They use the full arrangement of keys like the *normal type keyboard*

The keys are close together like on a *laptop keyboard*

Additionally, the flexibility of the keyboard allows the user to fold/roll it for better storage and transfer.

However, for typing, the keyboard must be resting on a hard surface.

The vast majority of flexible keyboards in the market are made from silicone; this material makes them water and dust proof, a very convenient feature, especially in hospitals where keyboards are subjected to frequent washing.

For connection with the computer the keyboards use a USB cable, and operating system support goes as far back as Windows 2000.

5.1.1.4 On-Screen Keyboards

Software keyboards, or on-screen keyboards, often take the form of computer programs that display an image of a keyboard on the screen. Another input device such as a mouse or a touchscreen can be used to operate each virtual key to enter text.

Software keyboards have become very popular in touchscreen enabled cell phones, since hardware keyboards cost more and occupy more physical space.

5.1.1.5 Projection Keyboards

Projection keyboards project an image of keys, usually with a laser, onto a flat surface. The device then uses a camera or infrared sensor to "watch" where the user's fingers move, and will count a key as being pressed when it "sees" the user's finger touch the projected image.

Projection keyboards can simulate a full-size keyboard from a very small projector.

Because the "keys" are simply projected images, they cannot be felt when pressed.

Users of projected keyboards often experience increased discomfort in their fingertips because of the lack of "give" when typing.

A flat, non-reflective surface is also required for the keys to be projected.

Most projection keyboards are made for use with PDAs and smartphones because their small size prohibits inclusion of physical keyboards.

5.1.2 Keyboard Layouts

There are a number of different arrangements of alphabetic, numeric, and punctuation symbols on keys.

These different keyboard layouts arise mainly because different people want easier access to different symbols, either because they are entering text in different languages, or because they need a specialized layout for mathematics, accounting, computer programming, or other purposes.

The United States keyboard layout is used as default in the currently most popular PC operating systems: Windows, Mac OS X and Linux.

5.1.2.1 QWERTY Keyboard

The common QWERTY-based layout was designed early in the era of mechanical typewriters, and its ergonomics were compromised to allow for the mechanical limitations of the typewriter.

As the letter-keys were attached to levers that needed to move freely, inventor Christopher Sholes developed the QWERTY layout to reduce the likelihood of jamming.

With the advent of computers, lever jams are no longer an issue, but nevertheless, QWERTY layouts were adopted for electronic keyboards because they were widely used.

Alternative layouts such as the *Dvorak Simplified Keyboard* are not in widespread use

5.1.2.2 Dvorak Simplified Keyboard

The [lxxi]**Dvorak Simplified Keyboard** is a keyboard layout patented in 1936 by Dr. August Dvorak and his brother-in-law, Dr. William Dealey.

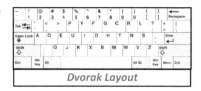
Dvorak Layout

Dvorak proponents claim the layout requires less finger motion and that its use results in fewer errors than the standard QWERTY layout. Its proponents also claim that the reduction in finger distance traveled permits faster rates of typing while also reducing repetitive strain injuries

5.1.2.3 Layouts for languages other than English

The QWERTZ layout is widely used in Germany and much of Central Europe. The main difference between QWERTZ and QWERTY is that Y and Z are swapped, and most special characters such as brackets are replaced by diacritical characters.

Another situation takes place with other "national" layouts. Keyboards designed for typing in Spanish have some characters shifted, to release the space for characters Ñ and ñ.

Similarly, those for Portuguese, French and other European languages may have a special key for the characters Ç and ç.

The AZERTY layout is used in France, Belgium and some neighboring countries. It differs from the QWERTY layout in that the A and Q are swapped, the Z and W are swapped, and the M is moved from the right of N to the right of L (where colon/semicolon is on a US keyboard). The digits 0 to 9 are on the same keys, but to be typed the shift key must be pressed. The unshifted positions are used for accented characters.

Keyboards in many parts of Asia may have special keys to switch between the Latin character set and a completely different typing system. Japanese layout keyboards can be switched between various Japanese input methods and the Latin alphabet by signaling the operating system's input interpreter of the change, and some operating systems (namely the Windows family) interpret the character "\" as "¥" for display purposes without changing the bytecode which has led some keyboard makers to mark "\" as "¥" or both.

In the Arab world, keyboards can often be switched between Arabic and Latin characters.

In bilingual regions of Canada and in the French-speaking province of Québec, keyboards can often be switched between an English and a French-language keyboard; while both keyboards share the same QWERTY alphabetic layout, the French-language keyboard enables the user to type accented vowels such as "é" or "à" with a single keystroke.

Using keyboards for more than one language leads to a conflict: the image on the key does not necessarily correspond to the character produced on the screen. In such cases, each new language may require an additional label on the keys, because the standard keyboard layouts do not share even similar characters of different languages

5.2 Scanners

An *image* scanner—usually abbreviated to just **scanner**—is a device that optically scans images and converts them to digital representations of the images. There are various kinds of scanners. Among them are:

[lxxii]*flatbed scanners* where the document is placed on a glass window for scanning.

[lxxiii]*Hand-held scanners*, where the scanning device is moved by hand

[lxxiv]*3D scanners* that are often used for industrial design, reverse engineering, test and measurement, gaming and other applications.

[lxxv]*Document scanners* are scanners designed specifically to process collections of loose leaf papers, usually just for text. These scanners generally have document feeders, usually larger than those sometimes found on copiers or all-purpose scanners. The main function of document scanners is to capture the images of scanned documents or text and save these images digitally to picture or PDF formats. With the advancement of scanning technology, most document scanners can distinguish variations in color. Those with built-in optical character recognition (OCR) software are able to convert images into editable text.

Scans on document scanners are made at high speed, perhaps 20 to 150 pages per minute, often in grayscale, although many document scanners do support color.

Many document scanners can scan both sides of double-sided originals (duplex operation). Sophisticated document scanners have firmware or software that cleans up scans of text as they are produced, eliminating accidental marks and sharpening type; this would be unacceptable for photographic work, where marks cannot reliably be distinguished from desired fine detail. Files created are compressed as they are made. The resolution used is usually from 150 to 300 dpi, although the hardware may be capable of somewhat higher resolution; this produces images of text good enough to read and for optical character recognition, without the higher demands on storage space required by higher-resolution images.

Optical character recognition (OCR) is the conversion of <u>images</u> of typed, handwritten or printed text into machine-encoded text, whether from a scanned document, a photo of a document, a scene-photo (for example the text on signs and billboards in a landscape photo) or from subtitle text superimposed on an image (for example from a television broadcast). It is widely used as a form of information entry from printed paper data records, whether passport documents, invoices, bank statements, computerized receipts, business cards, mail, printouts of static-data, or any suitable documentation. It is a common method of digitizing printed texts so that they can be electronically edited, searched, stored more compactly, displayed on-line, and used in machine processes

Color scanners that typically read RGB (red-green-blue color) data.

This data is processed with some proprietary algorithm to correct for different exposure conditions, and sent to the computer via the device's input/output interface (usually USB).

Color depth (the number of bits that a scanner uses to represent colors in its images) varies depending on the scanner, but is usually at least 24 bits. High quality models have 36-48 bits of color depth.

Another parameter used for describing the capabilities of scanners is *resolution*, measured in pixels per inch (ppi)

As of 2009, a high-end flatbed scanner could scan up to 5400 ppi and drum scanners had an optical resolution of between 3,000 and 24,000 ppi.

Flatbed Scanner

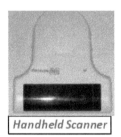
Handheld Scanner

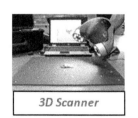
3D Scanner

Document scanner

5.3 Pointing Devices

A **pointing device** is an input interface that allows a user to communicate with a computer by controlling the position of a cursor on the computer display.

Although the most common pointing device is the mouse, many other devices have been developed as well. However, the term "mouse" is sometimes used as a generic term for a device that moves the cursor

5.3.1 Mouse

A **computer mouse**[lxxvi] is a pointing device. It is a small object you can roll along a hard, flat surface. This motion is translated into the movement of the cursor, and allows a smooth control of the graphical user interface.

Mouse

Invented by Douglas Engelbart of Stanford Research Center in 1963, and pioneered by Xerox in the 1970s, the mouse is one of the great breakthroughs in computer interaction.

Physically, a mouse consists of an object held in one's hand, and normally has one or more buttons. Mice often also feature other elements, such as "wheels", which enable additional control and dimensional input.

The mouse is important for graphical user interfaces because you can simply *point to* options and objects (move the cursor over them) and click a mouse button.

Such applications are often called *point-and-click* programs.

The mouse is also useful for graphics programs that allow you to draw pictures by using the mouse like a pen, pencil, or paintbrush.

There are three basic types of mice

1. **Mechanical:** Has a rubber or metal ball on its underside that can roll in all directions. Mechanical sensors within the mouse detect the direction the ball is rolling and move the screen pointer accordingly.

2. **Opto-mechanical:** Same as a mechanical mouse, but uses optical sensors to detect motion of the ball.

3. **Optical:** Uses a laser to detect the mouse's movement. Optical mice have no mechanical moving parts. They respond more quickly and precisely than mechanical and opto-mechanical mice, but they are also more expensive.

5.3.2 Trackball

A [lxxvii]**trackball** is a pointing device consisting of a ball held by a socket containing sensors to detect a rotation of the ball —like an upside-down mouse with an exposed ball.

Trackball

The user rolls the ball with the thumb, fingers, or the palm of the hand to move a pointer.

At times, a mouse can reach an edge of its working area while the operator still wishes to move the screen pointer farther. With a trackball, the operator just continues rolling, whereas a mouse would have to be lifted and re-positioned.

Because trackballs for personal computers are stationary, they may require less space for operation than a mouse, and may be easier to use in confined or cluttered areas. They are often preferred in laboratory settings for this reason.

Many people with a mobility impairment use trackballs as an assistive technology input device.

Access to an alternative pointing device has become even more important for these people with the dominance of graphically-oriented operating systems.

Trackball users often state that they are not limited to using the device on a flat desk surface. Trackballs can be used while browsing a laptop in bed, or can be used remotely from an armchair to a PC playing a movie. They are also useful for computing on boats or other unstable platforms where a rolling deck could produce undesirable input

5.3.3 Joystick

A joystick is a lever that moves in all directions and controls the movement of the pointer/cursor. A joystick works very much like a mouse, except that with a mouse the cursor stops moving as soon as you stop moving the mouse, but with a joystick, the pointer continues moving in the direction the joystick is pointing. To stop the pointer, you must return the joystick to its upright position.

Joystick

Most joysticks include two buttons called *triggers*. Joysticks are used mostly for computer games (the idea is to emulate an aircraft flight control system), but they are also used occasionally for CAD/CAM systems and other applications.

Joysticks are also used for controlling machines such as cranes, trucks, underwater unmanned vehicles, wheelchairs, surveillance cameras, and zero turning radius lawn mowers.

5.3.4 Touchscreen

A touch screen is a computer display screen that is also an input device. The screens are sensitive to pressure;

a user interacts with the computer by touching pictures or words on the screen.

There are three types of touch screen technology:

Resistive: A resistive touch screen panel is coated with a thin metallic electrically conductive and resistive layer that causes a change in the electrical current which is registered as a touch event and sent to the controller for processing. Resistive touch screen panels are generally more affordable but offer only 75% clarity and the layer can be damaged by sharp objects. Resistive touch screen panels are not affected by outside elements such as dust or water.

Surface wave: Surface wave technology uses ultrasonic waves that pass over the touch screen panel. When the panel is touched, a portion of the wave is absorbed. This change in the ultrasonic waves registers the position of the touch event and sends this information to the controller for processing. Surface wave touch screen panels are the most advanced of the three types, but they can be damaged by outside elements.

Capacitive: A capacitive touch screen panel is coated with a material that stores electrical charges. When the panel is touched, a small amount of charge is drawn to the point of contact. Circuits located at each corner of the panel measure the charge and send the information to the controller for processing. Capacitive touch screen panels must be touched with a finger unlike resistive and surface wave panels that can use fingers and stylus. Capacitive touch screens are not affected by outside elements and have high clarity.

5.3.5 Graphics Tablet

A [lxxviii]**graphic tablet** (also known as a **digitizer**, **drawing tablet**, **digital drawing tablet**, **pen tablet**, or **digital art board**) is a computer input device that enables a user to hand-draw images, animations and graphics, with a special pen-like stylus, similar to the way a person draws images with a pencil and paper.

graphics tablet

These tablets may also be used to capture data or handwritten signatures.

They can also be used to trace images from pieces of paper taped or otherwise secured to a tablet surface.

Capturing data in this way, by tracing or entering the corners of linear poly-lines or shapes, is called *digitizing*.

The device consists of a flat surface upon which the user may "draw" or trace an image using the attached stylus, a pen-like drawing apparatus. The image is displayed on the computer monitor, though some graphic tablets now also incorporate an LCD screen for a more realistic or natural experience and usability.

Some tablets are intended as a replacement for the computer mouse as the primary pointing and navigation device for desktop computers.

5.3.6 Touchpad

A **touchpad** or *trackpad* is a pointing device featuring a specialized surface that can sense the position (and movement) of the user's fingers touching it, and translate their motion and position to a relative position to be displayed on the screen.

Touchpads are a common feature of laptop computers, and are also used as a substitute for a mouse where desk space is scarce.

5.4 Speech Recognition

From the very first computers, workers have dreamed of being able to control computers by spoken commands. Until VERY recently, this was nothing more than a dream.

Recently, however, speech recognition has developed to where it can be used effectively, and its applications have become quite widespread, especially in business call centers.

Speech recognition technology still has a few issues to work through, and is still being continuously developed. The pros of speech recognition software are that it is easy to use and readily available.

Speech recognition software is now frequently installed in computers and mobile devices, allowing for easy access.

At present, the downside of speech recognition includes its inability to capture words due to variations of pronunciation, its lack of support for most languages outside of English and its inability to sort through background noise. These factors can lead to inaccuracies.

From the technology perspective, speech recognition has a long history with several waves of major innovations. Most recently, the field has benefited from advances in deep learning and big data. The advances are evidenced by the worldwide industry adoption and deployment of a variety of speech recognition systems. These speech industry players include Google, Microsoft, IBM, Baidu, Apple, Amazon, Nuance, SoundHound and iFLYTEK.

Much of the progress in the field is owed to the rapidly increasing capabilities of computers. At the end of an influential DARPA program in 1976, the best computer available to researchers was the PDP-10 with 4 MB ram. Using these computers it could take up to 100 minutes to decode just 30 seconds of speech. A few decades later, researchers had access to tens of thousands of times as much computing power. As the technology advanced and computers got faster, researchers began tackling harder problems such as larger vocabularies, speaker independence, noisy environments and conversational speech.

The 1990s saw the first introduction of commercially successful speech recognition technologies. Two of the earliest products were Dragon Dictate, a consumer product released in 1990 and originally priced at $9,000, and a recognizer from Kurzweil Applied Intelligence released in 1987. AT&T deployed the Voice Recognition Call Processing service in 1992 to route telephone calls without the use of a human operator. The technology was developed by Bell Labs. At that point, the vocabulary of the typical commercial speech recognition system was larger than the average human vocabulary.

In the United States, the National Security Agency has made use of a type of speech recognition for keyword spotting since at least 2006. This technology allows analysts to search through large volumes of recorded conversations and isolate mentions of keywords.

Neural networks have been used in many aspects of speech recognition such as phoneme classification, isolated word recognition, audiovisual speech recognition, audiovisual speaker recognition and speaker adaptation

Speech recognition is now widely used in:

- automobiles (Simple voice commands may be used to initiate phone calls, select radio stations or play music from a compatible smartphone, MP3 player or music-loaded flash drive)

- medical documentation (speech recognition can be implemented in front-end or back-end of the medical documentation process. Front-end speech recognition is where the provider dictates into a speech-recognition engine, the recognized words are displayed as they are spoken, and the dictator is responsible for editing and signing off on the document. Back-end or deferred speech recognition is where the provider dictates into a digital dictation system, the voice is routed through a speech-recognition machine and the recognized draft document is routed along with the original voice file to the editor, where the draft is edited and report finalized. Deferred speech recognition is widely used in the industry currently)

- telephony (speech recognition is now commonplace In the field of telephony, and is becoming more widespread in the field of computer gaming and simulation)

- education (speech recognition can be useful for learning a second language. It can teach proper pronunciation, in addition to helping a person develop fluency with their speaking skills.)

5.5 Questions

5.5.1 Completion

5. Examples of _____ devices include keyboards, mouse, scanners, digital cameras and joysticks

5. In computing, an **input device** is a(n) _____ (piece of computer hardware equipment) used to provide data and control signals *into* a computer

5.1 In computing, a **computer keyboard** is a(n) _____-style device which uses an arrangement of buttons or keys to act as electronic switches

5.1 In normal usage, the keyboard is used as a(n) _____ entry interface

5.1.1.3 The vast majority of flexible keyboards in the market are made from _____

5.1.1.5 _____ keyboards display an image of keys, usually with a laser, onto a flat surface. The device then uses a camera or infrared sensor to "watch" where the user's fingers move, and will count a key as being pressed when it "sees" the user's finger touch the projected image

5.1.2.1 The common _____-based layout was designed early in the era of mechanical typewriters, so its ergonomics were compromised to allow for the mechanical limitations of the typewriter

5.1.2.2 Proponents of the _____ keyboard claim the layout requires less finger motion and reduces errors compared to the standard layout

5.2 An *image* _____ is a device that optically scans images and converts them to digital representations of the images

5.3.5 Capturing data with a graphics tablet, by tracing or entering the corners of linear poly-lines or shapes, is called _____

5.4.2 Multiple Choice

5. A _____ is an example of an input device
   a) keyboard
   b) mouse
   c) scanner
   d) all of the above
   e) none of the above

5.1 A command-line interface is a type of user interface operated entirely through
_____
   a) keyboard
   b) voice command
   c) touchscreen
   d) any of the above
   e) none of the above

5.1.1.1 There are three different PC keyboards: The three differ somewhat in the placement of:
   a) the function keys
   b) the control keys
   c) the return key
   d) all of the above
   e) none of the above

5.1.1.4 Software keyboards have become very popular in touchscreen enabled cell phones, due to_____.
   a) their popularity among users who use them for games
   b) the additional cost and space requirements of other types of hardware keyboards
   c) the ease with which they can be reprogrammed for different languages
   d) all of the above
   e) none of the above

5.1.1.4 _____ keyboards have become very popular for cell phones, due to the additional cost and space requirements of other types of hardware keyboards
   a) Projection
   b) Flexible
   c) Software
   d) all of the above
   e) none of the above

5.1.2 The United States keyboard layout is used as default in
   a) Windows
   b) Mac OS X
   c) Linux
   d) all of the above
   e) none of the above

5.1.2.3 The _____ keyboard layout is widely used in Germany and much of Central Europe
   a) QWERTZ
   b) DVORAK
   c) AZERTY
   d) QWERTY
   e) none of the above

5.1.2.3 The _____ keyboard layout is used in France, Belgium and some neighboring countries
a) QWERTZ
b) DVORAK
c) AZERTY
d) QWERTY
e) none of the above

5.2 An *image* scanner—usually abbreviated to just **scanner**—is a device that optically scans images and converts them to digital representations of the images. There are various kinds of scanners. Among them are:
_____scanners where the document is placed on a glass window for scanning
a) flatbed
b) window
c) document
d) industrial
e) none of the above

5.2 An *image* scanner—usually abbreviated to just **scanner**—is a device that optically scans images and converts them to digital representations of the images. There are various kinds of scanners. Among them are:
_____ *scanners* that are often used for industrial design, reverse engineering, test and measurement, gaming and other applications
a) flatbed
b) window
c) document
d) industrial
e) none of the above

5.3 A _____**device** is an input interface that allows a user to input spatial data to a computer by controlling the position of a cursor on the computer display
a) cursor
b) spatial
c) pointing
d) all of the above
e) none of the above

5.3.1 The most common pointing device is the _____
a) touchscreen
b) mouse
c) touchpad
d) trackball
e) none of the above

5.3.1 The optical mouse _____
   a) is cheaper than a mechanical mouse and responds more slowly
   b) is cheaper than a mechanical mouse and responds more quickly
   c) is more expensive than a mechanical mouse and responds more slowly
   d) is more expensive than a mechanical mouse and responds more quickly
   e) none of the above

5.3.2 A _____ is a pointing device consisting of a ball held by a socket containing sensors to detect a rotation of the ball about two axes
   a) touchscreen
   b) mouse
   c) touchpad
   d) trackball
   e) none of the above

5.3.4 A _____ touch screen panel is coated with a thin metallic electrically conductive and resistive layer that causes a change in the electrical current which is registered as a touch event
   a) resistive
   b) surface wave
   c) capacitive
   d) all of the above
   e) none of the above

5.3.4 A _____ touch screen panel is coated with a material that stores electrical charges. When the panel is touched, a small amount of charge is drawn to the point of contact. Circuits located at each corner of the panel measure the charge and send the information to the controller for processing
   a) resistive
   b) surface wave
   c) capacitive
   d) all of the above
   e) none of the above

5.3.6 _____ are a common feature of laptop computers, and are also used as a substitute for a mouse where desk space is scarce
   a) Touchscreens
   b) Touchpads
   c) Joysticks
   d) all of the above
   e) none of the above

5.4.3 True-False

5.1 A keyboard typically has characters engraved or printed on the keys and each press of a key typically corresponds to a single written symbol

5.1 Despite the development of alternative input devices, such as the mouse, touchscreen, pen devices, character recognition and voice recognition, the keyboard remains the most commonly used device for direct (human) input of alphanumeric data into computers

5.1.1.1 The IEEE has established a standard computer keyboard design that all manufacturers conform to.

5.1.1.2 Keyboards on laptops and notebook computers usually have a shorter travel distance for the keystroke, shorter over travel distance, but always have the same set of keys

5.2 There are a number of different arrangements of alphabetic, numeric, and punctuation symbols on keys of computer keyboards

5.2 Document scanners produce very high resolution images.

5..3.3 Most joysticks include buttons called *triggers*

5.3.4 Resistive touch screen panels are not affected by outside elements such as dust or water

5.3.4 Capacitive touch screens are not affected by outside elements and have high clarity

5.3.6 Touchpads are a quite expensive and are found only on high end laptop computers.

6 Output

After a computer executed a program, has processed some data, it will probably be desirable for the computer to produce some kind of tangible effect in the outside world; for it to produce some kind of **output.**

Users normally want to have some indication of what the computer is doing or has done.

Computers have come to be able to produce a number of different kinds of output. Some of the general classes of computer output include text, graphics, tactile, audio, and video.

Text consists of characters that are used to create words, sentences, and paragraphs.

Graphics are digital representations of nontext information such as drawings, charts, photographs, and animation.

Tactile output such as raised line drawings may be useful for some individuals who are blind.

Audio is music, speech, or any other sound.

Video consists of images played back at speeds to provide the appearance of full motion

The great majority of the output produced by computers can be divided into two classes: output that users can *see* and output that users can *hear*

6.1 Visual Output

The kinds of computer output that people can *see* can be subdivided again, into two different classes. We describe these as hard copy and soft copy

Output resulting in reasonably permanent visual effects (often ink) on a physical medium (usually paper) is described as hard copy

Output resulting in temporary visual effects, effects that disappear as soon as the computer moves on to computation of some other task, is described as soft copy.

6.1.1 Visual Devices: Soft Copy

The most common computer output device is the computer **monitor** (or computer *screen*.) The term *monitor* [also referred to as a **video display terminal (VDT)** and **video display unit (VDU)**] refers to a display screen for video images, (and the case that holds it.)

Monitors create a visual display for you to view from processed data.

They come in a variety of screen sizes and visual resolutions.

Most monitors are rectangular in shape. Their size is usually described as a number of inches (measured on diagonal – corner to corner.)

"Resolution" is a term used to describe the capacity of a screen to display a sharp clear image. The resolution can be described in terms of "pixel density" (dots per inch or dpi) or, more often, in term of the total screen area - the number of distinct pixels in each dimension that can be displayed.

There are two common types of modern computer monitors, cathode ray tube (CRT) and flat panel screen. More recently a newer type, organic light-emitting diode (OLED) has started becoming popular as well.

6.1.1.1 CRT Monitors

The early computer monitors were constructed like the early TVs, as a CRT (Cathode Ray Tube) with a fluorescent screen.

CRT Monitor

CRT monitors use phosphorescent dots to create the pixels that make up displayed images.

6.1.1.2 Flat Panel Monitors

Today, monitors are created using *flat panel display technology.*

The term[lxxix]**Flat panel technology** refers to a growing number of electronic visual display technologies. They are thinner and weigh much less than traditional CRT television sets and video displays. Flat panel display units are usually less than 10 centimeters (3.9 in.) thick.

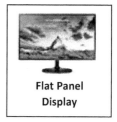

Flat Panel Display

Flat panel monitors usually create their displays using liquid crystals (LCD) but they can also use gas plasma.

6.1.1.2.1 LCD

Most of the modern flat-panel displays use **LCD** (liquid crystal display) technologies.

Light is passed through liquid crystals to create the pixels.

LCD screens are usually back-lit to make them easier to read in bright environments. They are thin and light and provide good linearity and resolution.

A thin layer of liquid crystal (a liquid having crystalline properties) is sandwiched between two electrically conducting plates. The front plate has transparent electrodes deposited on it, and the back plate is illuminated.

By applying electrical signals across the plates, different regions of the liquid crystal can be activated, to change their in their polarizing properties. These segments can either transmit or block light. An image is produced by passing light through selected segments of the liquid crystal to the viewer. They are used in various electronics like watches, cellphones, and calculators, as well as notebook computers.

Liquid crystal displays are lightweight, compact, portable and cheap and they are more reliable, and easier on the eyes than CRTs.

6.1.1.2.2 Gas Plasma

Very large displays often use *plasma display technology*.

A [lxxx]*plasma display* consists of two glass plates separated by a thin gap filled with a gas such as neon. Each of these plates has several parallel electrodes running across it. The electrodes on the two plates are at right angles to each other. A voltage applied between the two electrodes one on each plate causes a small segment of gas at the two electrodes to glow. The glow of gas segments is maintained by a lower voltage that is continuously applied to all electrodes.

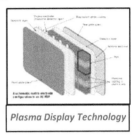

Plasma Display Technology

Advantages

- Capable of producing deeper blacks allowing for superior contrast ratio. Wider viewing angles than those of LCD;
- images do not suffer from degradation at less than straight ahead angles like LCDs
- Less visible motion blur, thanks in large part to very high refresh rates and a faster response time, contributing to superior performance when displaying content with significant amounts of rapid motion.
- Superior uniformity. LCD panel backlights nearly always produce uneven brightness levels, (although this is not always noticeable.)
- Less expensive for the buyer per square inch than LCD, particularly when equivalent performance is considered.

Disadvantages

- Earlier generation displays were more susceptible to screen burn-in and image retention.
- Due to the bistable nature of the color and intensity generating method, some people will notice that plasma displays have a shimmering or flickering effect with a number of hues, intensities and dither patterns.
- Earlier generation displays (circa 2006 and prior) had phosphors that lost luminosity over time, resulting in gradual decline of absolute image brightness. (Newer models have advertised lifespans exceeding 100 000 hours, far longer than older CRTs)
- Uses more electrical power, on average, than an LCD TV using a LED backlight. Older CCFL backlights for LCD panels used quite a bit more power, and older plasma TVs used quite a bit more power than recent models.

- Does not work as well at high altitudes above 6,500 feet (2,000 meters) due to pressure differential between the gasses inside the screen and the air pressure at altitude. It may cause a buzzing noise. Manufacturers rate their screens to indicate the altitude parameters.
- Plasma displays are generally heavier than LCD and may require more careful handling such as being kept upright.

Plasma displays have lost nearly all market share, mostly due to competition from low-cost LCD and more expensive but high-contrast OLED flat-panel displays. Manufacturing for the United States retail market ended in 2014.

6.1.1.3 Organic Light-Emitting Diode (OLED)

An **organic light-emitting diode (OLED)** is a light-emitting diode (LED) formed as a film of organic compound located between two electrodes.

OLED displays can be manufactured on flexible plastic leading to the possible production of *flexible* organic light-emitting diodes for new applications, such as roll-up displays and fabrics or clothing with embedded OLEDS.

OLEDs are sometimes used to create digital displays in devices such as television screens, computer monitors, and portable systems such as mobile phones, handheld game consoles and PDAs.

Because the substrate used can be flexible, they are also shatter resistant, unlike glass displays used in LCD devices

Flexible OLED's are also often used in *wearable* devices, because they are light weight and require little power (in addition to being flexible and capable of producing various colors.)

Wearable technology, **wearables**, **fashionable technology**, **wearable devices**, **tech togs**, or **fashion electronics** are clothing and accessories incorporating computer and advanced electronic technologies.

These designs often incorporate practical functions and features, but may also have a purely critical or aesthetic agenda.

Wearables make technology pervasive by interweaving it into daily life.

Throughout the history and development of wearable computing, pioneers have attempted to enhance or extend the functionality of clothing, or to create wearables as accessories able to provide users with the capacity to record their activities

(typically, by way of small wearable or portable personal technologies.)

Tracking information like movement, steps and heart rate are all part of quantifying self-movement.

One early piece of widely-adopted wearable technology was the [lxxxi]calculator watch, introduced in the 1980s.

Calculator Watch

6.1.1.4 Projectors

[lxxxii]A **projector** or **image projector** is an optical device that projects an image (or moving images) onto a surface (often a projection screen.)

The computer sends the image data to its video card, which then sends the video image to the projector.

Acer Projector

Projectors are typically used for presentations or for viewing videos.

Most projectors create an image by shining a light through a small transparent lens, but some newer types of projectors can project the image directly, by using lasers.

The most common type of projector used today is called a **video projector.**

Video projectors are digital replacements for earlier types of projectors such as slide projectors.

These earlier types of projectors were mostly replaced with digital video projectors throughout the 1990s and early 2000s, but old analog projectors are still used at some places.

The newest types of projectors are **handheld projectors** that use lasers or LEDs to project images.

Their projections are hard to see if there is too much ambient light.

Epson AAXA P700 Pocket Projector

6.1.1.5 Virtual Reality Headsets

[lxxxiii]A **virtual reality headset** is a head-mounted device that provides virtual reality for the wearer.

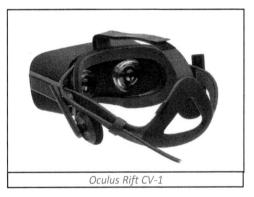

Virtual reality (VR) headsets are widely used with **video games** but they are also used in other applications, including simulators and trainers. They include a stereoscopic head-mounted display (with separate images for each eye), stereo sound, and head motion tracking sensors (which may include **gyroscopes, accelerometers, structured light** systems, etc.). Some VR headsets also have **eye tracking** sensors and **gaming controllers**.

Oculus Rift CV-1

6.1.2 Hard Copy devices - Printers

Printers produce a hard copy version of processed data such as documents and photographs. The computer sends the image data to the printer, which then physically recreates the image, usually on paper. There are three common types of computer printers: ink jet, laser and dot matrix.

Inkjet printers spray tiny dots of ink on a surface to create an image.

Laser printers use toner drums that roll through magnetized pigment and then transfer the pigment to a surface.

Dot matrix printers were common in the 1980s and 1990s. They use a print head to embed images on a surface, using an ink ribbon.

Dot Matrix Printer   *Inkjet Printer*   *Laser Printer*

6.1.2.1 Inkjet Printers

Inkjet printers have a number of advantages over other consumer-oriented printers. They are quieter in operation than impact dot matrix or daisywheel printers, and they can print finer, smoother details because they are capable of higher resolution. Consumer inkjet printers with photographic-quality printing are widely available.

Inkjet printers tend to be lower priced than laser printers, especially color laser printers, and are the type of printer most commonly found in homes and small offices.

Storage of inkjet documents can problematical, depending on the quality of the inks and paper used.

If low-quality paper is used, it can yellow and degrade due to residual acid in the untreated pulp;

in the worst case, old prints can literally crumble into small particles when handled.

Of course, this is a property of the paper, not the printer, and would be true for any kind of printer using this paper.

High-quality inkjet prints on acid-free paper can last as long as typewritten or handwritten documents on the same paper.

The ink used in many low-cost consumer inkjets is water-soluble, so care must be taken with inkjet-printed documents to avoid contact with moisture, which can cause severe "blurring" or "running".

In extreme cases, even sweaty fingertips during hot humid weather could cause low-quality inks to smear.

Similarly, water-based highlighter markers can blur inkjet-printed documents, and can also discolor the highlighter's tip.

Many inkjet printers now use pigment based inks which are highly water resistant. In some cases, only the black ink is pigment based.

Resin or silicone protected photopaper is widely available at low cost, introducing complete water and mechanical rub resistance for dye and pigment inks.

The photopaper itself must be designed for pigment or for dye inks, as pigment particles are too large to be able to penetrate through dye-only photopaper protection layer.

6.1.2.2 [lxxxiv]Laser Printers

Laser printing is an electrostatic digital printing process. It produces high-quality text and graphics (but only moderate-quality photographs) by passing a laser beam back and forth over a charged cylinder (called a "drum") to create an electrostatic representation of the desired image.

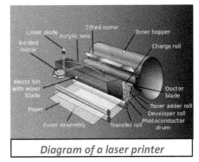

Diagram of a laser printer

The drum then attracts electrically charged powdered ink (called toner) and transfers the image to paper. The paper is then heated in order to fuse the ink onto the paper.

Laser printing differs from other printing technologies in that each page is always rendered in a single continuous process without any pausing in the middle. Other technologies, like inkjet, can pause every few lines. A laser printer needs enough memory to hold the bitmap image of an entire page.

Memory requirements increase with the *square* of the dots per inch.

During the 1980s, memory chips were still very expensive, which is why, at that time, entry-level laser printers came with four-digit retail prices. Later, memory prices plunged, and 1200 dpi laser printers have been widely available in the consumer market since 2008.

Laser printers that print on plastic sheets, are also available.

6.1.2.3 Dot Matrix Printers

[lxxxv]**Dot matrix printing** or **impact matrix printing** is a kind of computer printing that uses a print head that pushes wires against an ink-soaked cloth ribbon to make dots on the paper. Letters are drawn out of a dot matrix, and varied fonts, as well as arbitrary graphics can be produced.

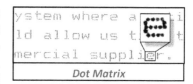
Dot Matrix

Each dot is produced by a tiny metal rod, also called a "wire" or "pin", which is extruded from the print head by the power of a tiny electromagnet or solenoid.

In the 1970s and 1980s, dot matrix impact printers were generally considered the best combination of expense and versatility, and until the 1990s they were by far the most common form of printer used with personal and home computers. They are not, however, very quiet.

Dot matrix printers are still preferred where fan fold paper is desired and/or where there is a requirement for multiple copies (since non-impact printers do not support carbon copies.)

6.1.2.4 Other Kinds of Printers

6.1.2.4.1 Virtual Printers

A *virtual printer* is a piece of computer software that acts like a printer driver, but which is not connected with a physical computer printer. Instead, a virtual printer can be used to create a file which is an image of the data which would be printed. These files can be used for archival purposes or as input to another program (in format of a PDF file, for example) or to transmit to another system or user.

6.1.2.4.2 3D Printers

A *3D printer* is a device for making a three-dimensional object from a 3D model or other electronic data source. 3D printers place layers of material (including plastics, metals, food, cement, wood, and other materials) one over another under computer control. They work in much the same way that an inkjet printer deposits layers of ink on paper.

6.1.2.4.3 Solid ink printers

Solid ink printers (also known as phase-change printers) are a type of thermal transfer printer. They use solid sticks of colored ink, similar in consistency to candle wax. These sticks are melted and fed into a print-head. The printhead sprays the ink on a rotating, oil coated drum. The paper then passes over the print drum and the image is transferred to the page.

Solid ink printers are most commonly used as color printers in offices. They are excellent at printing on transparencies and other non-porous media. Solid ink printers can produce excellent results. Their acquisition and operating costs are similar to laser printers.

Drawbacks of the technology include high energy consumption and long warm-up times. Also, some users complain that the resulting prints are difficult to write on, because the wax tends to repel inks. This type of printer is only available from one manufacturer, Xerox, manufactured as part of their Xerox Phaser office printer line.

6.1.2.4.4 Dye-sublimation printers

A dye-sublimation printer (or dye-sub printer) is a printer which employs a printing process that uses heat to transfer dye to a medium such as a plastic card, paper or canvas. The process is usually to lay one color at a time using a ribbon that has color panels.

Dye-sub printers are intended primarily for high-quality color applications, including color photography; and are less well-suited for text. Dye-sublimation printers are now increasingly used as dedicated consumer photo printers.

6.1.2.4.5 Thermal printers

Thermal printers work by selectively heating regions of special heat-sensitive paper.

Thermal printers are widely used in cash registers, ATMs, gasoline dispensers and some older inexpensive fax machines.

Thermal printer

Colors can be achieved with special papers and different temperatures and heating rates for different colors.

Output tends to fade over time.

6.1.2.4.6 Daisy Wheel Printers

[lxxxvi]Daisy wheel printers operate in much the same fashion as a typewriter. A hammer strikes a wheel with petals, the "daisy wheel", each petal containing a letter form at its tip. The letter form strikes a ribbon of ink, depositing the ink on the page and thus printing a character. By rotating the daisy wheel, different characters are selected for printing. These printers were also referred to as *letter-quality printers* because they could produce text which was as clear and crisp as a typewriter. The fastest letter-quality printers printed at 30 characters per second.

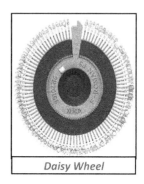

Daisy Wheel

By 1980 daisy wheel printers had become the dominant technology for high-quality print. Dot-matrix impact, thermal, or line printers were used where higher speed was required and poor print quality was acceptable. Both technologies were rapidly superseded for most purposes when dot-based printers—in particular laser and ink jet printers—that could print any characters or graphics, rather than being restricted to a limited character set, became able to produce output of comparable quality

6.1.2.4.7 Plotters

Pen-based **plotters** were an alternate printing technology once common in engineering and architectural firms.

Pen-based plotters rely on contact with the paper (but not impact, per se) and special purpose pens that are mechanically run over the paper to create text and images. Since the pens output continuous lines, they were able to produce technical drawings of higher resolution than was achievable with dot-matrix technology.

Some plotters used roll-fed paper, and therefore had minimal restriction on the size of the output in one dimension. These plotters were capable of producing quite sizable drawings.

6.1.3 Visual Output - Fonts

A great deal of computer generated information is displayed as *text*, whether on a monitor (referred to as *soft copy*, because it very quickly disappears, leaving no permanent record) or on paper, printed by a printer (referred to as *hard copy* because there is a physical record of what was printed.)

Text can be printed in various sizes and styles/fonts

Technically, the term "font" refers to a combination of three things: font-face, font-style and font-size, but the word is frequently used to mean just font-face.

6.1.3.1 Font-Face

The font-face (typeface) is the general appearance of the characters, ie. What they look like, how they are shaped.

There are two general classifications of fonts: serif and san-serif. A **serif** is a small line attached to the end of a stroke in a letter or symbol A typeface with serifs is called a **serif typeface** (or **serifed typeface**). A typeface without serifs is called sans serif or sans-serif. There is considerable debate as to which type of font face is easier to read. There are studies to support both sides of the issue.

One of the most common serif fonts is named **Times-New-Roman**

0123456789abcdxyzABCDXYZ

A commonly used san-serif font is named Ariel

0123456789abcdxyzABCDXYZ

6.1.3.2 Font-Style

The term "**font-style**" refers to whether a font is printed/displayed using any of a few properties (each of which can be used in combination with any, or all, of the others):

Bold

Italicized

<u>Underlined</u>

6.1.3.3 Font-Size

The **font size** (or **text size**) is the overall size (generally height) of a font shown on a screen or printed on a page.

A font is typically measured in **points** (**pt**).

This is the vertical measurement of the lettering.

There are approximately 72 points in one inch. (Points were, more or less, inherited from physical typography and referred to the smallest unit that could be printed. The standard for computer use was defined by Adobe when developing Adobe Postscript.)

Although *points* are the traditional measurement of fonts, with computer monitors and other kinds of screen displays font sizes can also be measured in **pixels** (**px**) and in **pica** (**pc**).

The font size may also be measured in em space, which is the width of the character m in the current font. (The em measurement is convenient for defining sizes of individual characters relative to characters around them.)

6.2 Audio Output

Computers produce *audio data* that requires output devices such as **speakers** and **headphones** to deliver the sound to you.

A **computer speaker** is a hardware device that connects to a computer to generate sound. The signal used to produce the sound that comes from a computer speaker is often created by the computer's sound card

Headphones are a pair of small listening devices that are designed to be worn on or around the head over a user's ears. They convert an electrical signal to a corresponding sound in the user's ear.

[lxxxvii]Headphones are designed to allow a single user to listen to an audio source privately, in contrast to a speaker, which emits sound into the open air, for anyone nearby to hear.

Circumaural and supra-aural headphones use a band over the top of the head to hold the speakers in place.

An alternative type of headphones, known as **earbuds** or **earphones,** [l]consist of individual units that plug into the user's ear canal.

In the context of telecommunication, a **headset** is a combination of a headphone and a microphone

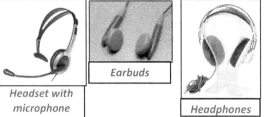

Headset with microphone

Earbuds

Headphones

Computer Speakers

6.3 Questions

6.3.1 Completion

6. After a computer executed a program, has processed some data, it will probably be desirable for the computer to produce some kind of tangible effect in the outside world; for it to produce some kind of _____

6.1.1 A(n) _____ creates a visual display for you to view from processed data

6.1.1.2.2 A(n) _____ *display* consists of two glass plates separated by a thin gap filled with a gas such as neon

6.1.1.3 A(n) _____ is a light-emitting diode (LED) in which the emissive electroluminescent layer is a film of organic compound that emits light in response to an electric current.

6.1.1.3 Flexible OLED's are often used in _____ devices

6.1.1.4 Most projectors create an image by shining a light through a small transparent lens, but some newer types of projectors can project the image directly, by using _____

6.1.2.2 _____ printing differs from other printing technologies in that each page is always rendered in a single continuous process without any pausing in the middle, while other technologies like inkjet can pause every few lines.

6.1.2.4.1 A(n) _____ *printer* is a piece of computer software whose user interface and API resembles that of a printer driver, but which is not connected with a physical computer printer. It can be used to create a file which is an image of the data which would be printed, for archival purposes or as input to another program

6.1.2.4.5 _____ printers are widely used in cash registers, ATMs, gasoline dispensers and some older inexpensive fax machines.

6.1.2.4.7 Pen-based _____ were an alternate printing technology once common in engineering and architectural firms

6.1.3.1 A(n) _____ is a small line attached to the end of a stroke in a letter or symbol

6.1.3.3 There are approximately _____ points in one inch

6.2 _____are designed to allow a single user to listen to an audio source privately, in contrast to a speaker, which emits sound into the open air, for anyone nearby to hear

6.2 An alternative type of headphones, known as _____or **earphones,** consist of individual units that plug into the user's ear canal

6.2 In the context of telecommunication, a _____is a combination of a headphone and a microphone

6.3.2 Multiple Choice

6.1.1 A *VDU* is:
a) a monitor
b) a printer
c) a wearable
d) a speaker
e) none of the above

6.1.1 A *VDT* is:
a) a monitor
b) a printer
c) a wearable
d) a speaker
e) none of the above

6.1.1.3 Flexible OLED's, which are often used in *wearable* devices,
a) are relatively heavy and are somewhat power hungry
b) are light weight but are somewhat power hungry
c) are relatively heavy but require little power
d) are light weight and require little power
e   none of the above

6.1.1.4 The newest type of projectors is _____ projector
a) wearable
b) laser
c) handheld
d) color
e) none of the above

6.1.2 _____ **printers** spray tiny dots of ink on a surface to create an image
a) inkspray
b) inkjet
c) inkdot
d) spraydot
e) none of the above

6.1.2.2 _____ printing differs from other printing technologies in that each page is always rendered in a single continuous process without any pausing in the middle, while other technologies can pause every few lines
a) Dot matrix
b) Inkjet
c) Laser
d) Thermal
e) none of the above

6.1.2.3 _____ printing is a type of computer printing which uses a print head that prints by impact, striking an ink-soaked cloth ribbon against the paper
a) Dot matrix
b) Inkjet
c) Laser
d) Thermal
e) none of the above

6.1.2.3 In the 1970s and 1980s, _____ printers were generally considered the best combination of expense and versatility, and until the 1990s they were by far the most common form of printer used with personal and home computers
a) Dot matrix
b) Inkjet
c) Laser
d) Thermal
e) none of the above

6.1.2.4.3 _____ printers are most commonly used as color office printers, and are excellent at printing on transparencies and other non-porous media
a) Dot matrix
b) Inkjet
c) Laser
d) Thermal
e) none of the above

6.1.3.3 The **font size** (or **text size**) is the overall size (generally height) of a font shown on a screen or printed on a page. A font is typically measured in:
a) pt
b) px
c) pc
d) em
e) none of the above

6.1.2.4.4 _____ printers are now increasingly used as dedicated consumer photo printers
a) Dot matrix
b) Inkjet
c) Laser
d) Thermal
e) none of the above

6.1.2.4.5 _____ printers are widely used in cash registers, ATMs, gasoline dispensers and some older inexpensive fax machines
a) Dot matrix
b) Inkjet
c) Laser
d) Thermal
e) none of the above

6.1.2.4.6 These printers were also referred to as *letter-quality printers* because they could produce text which was as clear and crisp as a typewriter.
a) dye-sub
b) daisy-wheel
c) dot-matrix
d) thermal
e) none of the above

6.3.3 True-False

6.1.1.2.2 Very large displays generally use ***plasma display technology***

6.1.1.2.2 CRT screens are usually back-lit to make them easier to read in bright environments.

6.1.1.2.2 Liquid crystal displays are lightweight, compact, portable and cheap and they are also more reliable than CRTs.

6.1.1.4 The newest handheld projectors produce images that are easy to see, even when there is ambient light.

6.1.2.1 Consumer inkjet printers with photographic-quality printing are widely available

6.1.2.1 Inkjet printers tend to be lower priced than color laser printers

6.1.3.1 There is considerable debate as to which type of font, serif or sans-serif, is easier to read. There are studies to support both sides of the issue

6.1.3.1 Times-New-Roman is an example of a font style.

6.1.3.1 The text in this question is displayed using a *serif* font.

7 Storage

Computer data storage, often called **storage** or **memory**, is a technology consisting of computer components and recording media used to retain digital data. It is a core function and fundamental component of computers.

In practice, almost all computers use a storage hierarchy, which puts fast but expensive (and small) storage options close to the CPU and slower but larger and cheaper options farther away.

Generally, the fast but *volatile* technologies (which lose data when power is turned off) are referred to as "memory", while slower persistent technologies are referred to as "storage"; or "secondary storage".

Secondary storage (also known as external memory or auxiliary storage), also differs from primary storage in that it is not directly accessible by the CPU.

The computer usually uses its input/output channels to access secondary storage and transfers the desired data into and out of intermediate areas (buffers) in primary storage (memory/RAM).

Secondary storage does not lose the data when the device is powered down—it is *non-volatile*.

It is typically also two orders of magnitude less expensive than primary storage (memory/RAM).

Modern computer systems typically have two orders of magnitude more secondary storage than primary storage.

In modern computers, hard disk drives are by far the most common form of secondary storage. Some other examples of secondary storage technologies are optical disk drives, flash memory (e.g. USB flash drives or keys), floppy disks, magnetic tape, paper tape, punched cards, standalone RAM disks, and Iomega Zip drives.

7.1 Hard disk drives

[lxxxviii]A **hard disk drive (HDD)**, **hard disk**, **hard drive** or **fixed disk** is a data storage device used for storing and retrieving digital information using one or more rigid ("hard") rapidly rotating disks (called *platters*) coated with magnetic material.

Hard Disk Drive
With cover removed

The platters are paired with magnetic heads arranged on a movable actuator arm. These heads can read and write data to the platter surfaces.

The surfaces of each disk are divided into circular "tracks" and each track is subdivided into a number of "sectors". The actuator arm can move relatively quickly to the track where given data is (or is to be) stored, and then the disk will rotate to where the appropriate sector passes by the read/write head. This technology, then, supports "random-access" for the data.

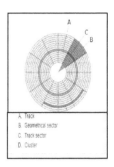

A. Track
B. Geometrical sector
C. Track sector
D. Cluster

(meaning that individual blocks of data can be stored or retrieved in any order rather than sequentially.)

The time taken to access a given byte of information stored on a hard disk is typically a few milliseconds (thousandths of a second.)

By contrast, the time taken to access a given byte of information stored in RAM (random-access memory) is measured in nanoseconds (billionths of a second.) This illustrates the significant difference in access-time between solid-state memory and rotating magnetic storage devices: hard disks are typically about a million times slower than RAM.

With disk drives, once the disk read/write head reaches the proper placement and the data of interest rotates under it, subsequent data on the track are much faster to access.

The time it takes to move the head to the proper placement is called "seek time".

The time it takes for the desired data to rotate under the head is called "rotational latency"

To reduce the seek time and rotational latency, data are transferred to and from disks in large contiguous blocks.

Sequential or block access on disks is orders of magnitude faster than random access, and many sophisticated paradigms have been developed to design efficient algorithms based upon sequential and block access

The two most common form factors for modern HDDs are 3.5-inch, for desktop computers, and 2.5-inch, primarily for laptops. HDDs are connected to systems by standard interface cables such as PATA (Parallel ATA), SATA (Serial ATA), USB or SAS (Serial attached SCSI) cables.

Introduced by IBM in 1956, HDDs became the dominant secondary storage device for general-purpose computers by the early 1960s. Continuously improved, HDDs have maintained this position into the modern era.

As the 1980s began, HDDs were a rare and very expensive additional feature in PCs, but by the late 1980s their cost had been reduced to the point where they had become standard on all but the cheapest computers.

Most HDDs in the early 1980s were sold to PC end users as an external, add-on subsystem. The subsystem was not sold under the drive manufacturer's name but under the subsystem manufacturer's name such as Corvus Systems and Tallgrass Technologies, or under the PC system manufacturer's name such as the Apple ProFile. The IBM PC/XT in 1983 included an internal 10 MB HDD, and soon thereafter internal HDDs became much more common on personal computers.

7.1.1 RAID

Random Array of Inexpensive Disks

When relatively inexpensive, albeit smaller and, in many cases less reliable, hard disks started to be marketed, it was recognized that by using several smaller hard disks instead of just one large disk, one could use a collection of smaller less expensive disks to create a *system* having a large capacity. Such a system could have several advantages:

Price: It was usually possible to buy large storage capacity for less money as a combination of smaller cheaper drives than a single high capacity drive would cost, since the smaller drives were manufactured in large quantities, resulting in economies of scale. The smaller drives were also more readily available.

Reliability: With several different drives, it is possible to put duplicate data on more than one drive. Then, if one drive were to fail, its data would not be lost.

Access Speed: With data in a large file stored on different drives, the system can read different portions of the file from the different drives simultaneously, resulting in faster upload times than would be possible with one single drive.

In a RAID system, data can be distributed across the drives in several different ways, referred to as RAID levels. These levels vary according to the required level of redundancy and performance.

The different schemes, or data distribution layouts, are named by the word RAID followed by a number, for example RAID 0 or RAID 1.

Each scheme, or RAID level, provides a different balance among the key goals: reliability, availability, performance, and capacity.

RAID levels greater than RAID 0 provide protection against unrecoverable sector read errors, as well as against failures of whole physical drives

7.1.2 Data Compression

Because in the early days of computing, storage was expensive (and limited) a number of techniques were developed, and several programs were marketed for compression of files (and collections of files) to create files having all of the information from the originals but requiring much less storage space. The most widely used programs produce (and interpret) compressed files have file extensions zip and rar.

The price of storage has come down, and capacities have increased radically over time, but data compression has continued to be important. The speed at which data can be transferred is critical in many areas of application, and, obviously, if the information can be represented using fewer bits (in a compressed format) then it can be transmitted in less time (i.e. faster.)

7.2 Optical Storage Devices

[lxxxix]**Optical storage** is the storage of data on an optically readable medium. Data is recorded by making marks in a pattern that can be read back using light, usually a beam of laser light, precisely focused on a spinning optical disc.

Rotating optical storage devices, such as CD and DVD drives, have even longer access times than do hard disk drives.

CD/DVD Disk Drive

The three most common optical media are CD, DVD and Blu-ray. CDs store about 300,000 pages of text or roughly 700 MB. DVDs are commonly used for movies and hold around 4.7 GB of memory. Blu-ray has five times the storage of DVD and is used for high-definition (HD) movies. On a single-layer disc, Blu-ray can hold 25GB of data, and a dual-layer disc can hold 9 hours of an HD movie or about 50GB of data.

Optical discs can be used to backup relatively small volumes of data, but backing up of entire hard drives, which as of 2015 typically contain many hundreds of gigabytes or even multiple terabytes, is less practical. Large backups are often instead made on external hard drives, since their price has dropped to a level making this viable; in professional environments. Magnetic tape drives are also used.

7.3 Flash Memory

[xc]**Flash memory** (e.g. USB flash drives or keys) A **USB flash drive**, also variously known as a **USB drive**, **USB stick**, **thumb drive**, **pen drive**, **jump drive**, **flash-disk**, "**memory stick**," or **USB memory**, is a data storage device that includes solid state (flash) memory with an integrated USB interface. USB flash drives are typically removable and rewritable, and physically much smaller than an optical disc. Most weigh less than 30 grams (1.1 oz).

Flash Drive

Since they first appeared on the market in late 2000, storage capacities have risen and prices have dropped.

As of March 2016, flash drives with anywhere from 8 to 256 GB are frequently sold, and less frequently 512 GB and 1 TB units. Storage capacities as large as 2 TB are planned, with steady improvements in size and price per capacity expected.

USB flash drives are often used for the same purposes for which floppy disks or CDs were once used, i.e., for storage, data back-up and transfer of computer files.

They are smaller, faster, have thousands of times more capacity, and are more durable and reliable because they have no moving parts.

Additionally, they are immune to electromagnetic interference (unlike floppy disks) and are unharmed by surface scratches (unlike CDs).

Until about 2005, most desktop and laptop computers were supplied with floppy disk drives in addition to USB ports, but floppy disk drives have become obsolete after widespread adoption of USB ports and the larger USB drive capacity compared to the floppy disk.

7.4 Obsolete Media

There are a number of types of storage media that were common at one time but are no longer widely used.

7.4.1 Floppy Disks

[xci]A **floppy disk**, also called a **floppy**, a **diskette** or just **disk**, is a type of disk storage composed of a disk of thin and flexible magnetic storage medium, sealed in a rectangular plastic enclosure lined with fabric that removes dust particles. Floppy disks are read and written by a **floppy disk drive** (FDD).

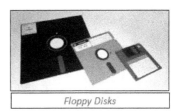
Floppy Disks

Floppy disks, initially as 8-inch (200 mm) media and later in 5¼-inch (133 mm) and even later in 3½-inch (90 mm) sizes, were a very widely used form of data storage and exchange from the mid-1970s into the late 2000s.

7.4.2 Magnetic Tape

[xcii]**Magnetic tape** is a medium for magnetic recording, made of a thin, magnetizable coating on a long, narrow strip of plastic film. It was a key technology in early computer development, allowing unparalleled amounts of data to be mechanically created, stored for long periods, and to be rapidly accessed.

Magnetic Tape

Tape remains a viable alternative to disk in some situations due to its lower cost per bit. This is a big advantage when dealing with large amounts of data. Though the areal density of tape is lower than for disks, the available surface area on a tape is far greater. The highest capacity tape media are generally on the same order as the largest available disk drives (about 5 TB in 2011).

Tape has historically offered enough advantage in cost to make it a viable alternative to disk storage, particularly for backup, where media removability is necessary.

121

7.4.3 Punched Paper Tape

[xciii]**Punched tape** or **perforated paper tape** is a form of data storage, consisting of a long strip of paper in which holes are punched to store data. Now effectively obsolete, it was widely used during much of the twentieth century for teleprinter communication, and, somewhat later, for input to computers of the 1950s and 1960s, and even later as a storage medium for minicomputers.

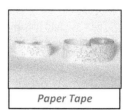

Paper Tape

When the first minicomputers were being released, most manufacturers turned to the existing mass-produced ASCII teleprinters (primarily the Teletype Model 33) as a low-cost solution for keyboard input and printer output.

The commonly specified Model 33 ASR included a paper tape punch/reader, (where ASR stands for "Automatic Send/Receive") as opposed to the punchless/readerless KSR – (Keyboard Send/Receive) and RO – (Receive Only) models.

As a side effect, punched tape became a popular medium for low cost minicomputer data and program storage, and it was common to find a selection of tapes containing useful programs in most minicomputer installations. Faster optical readers for paper tape were also common.

7.4.4 Punched Cards

[xciv]**Punched cards** were widely used through much of the 20th century in what became known as the *data processing* industry, where specialized and increasingly complex machines, organized into data processing systems, used punched cards for data input, output, and storage.

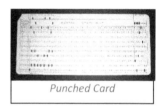

Punched Card

Herman Hollerith invented the recording of data on a medium that could then be read by a machine. (Prior uses of machine readable media had been for control, not data). After some initial trials with paper tape, he settled on punched cards, developing punched card data processing technology for the 1890 US census, and forming a company that was later to become (a major part of) what would become known as IBM.

Punched card technology developed into a powerful tool for business data-processing. By 1950 punched cards had become ubiquitous in industry and government.

Most early digital computers used punched cards as the primary medium for input of both computer programs and data These were often prepared using specialized *keypunch* machines

7.4.5 Zip Drive

[xcv]The **Zip drive** is a removable floppy disk storage system that was introduced by Iomega in late 1994. At the time of its release it was a medium-to-high-capacity device.

Zip Drive

Originally, Zip disks launched with capacities of 100 MB, but later versions increased this to 250 MB and, even later, to 750 MB.

The format became the most popular of the "superfloppy" products which filled a niche in the portable storage market in the late 1990s.

However, it was never popular enough to replace the 3.5-inch floppy disk. Later versions of the disc matched the capacity available on rewritable CDs but this was later far surpassed by rewritable DVDs

Zip drives fell out of favor for mass portable storage during the early 2000s

7.5 Cloud Storage

Some organizations have begun renting storage to subscribers.

Referred to as "cloud storage" or "storage in the cloud"

Cloud storage is a model of data storage in which the digital data is stored in logical pools. The physical storage spans multiple servers (and often locations), and the physical environment is typically owned and managed by a hosting company.

These cloud storage providers are responsible for keeping the data available and accessible, and the physical environment protected and running.

People and organizations buy or lease storage capacity from the providers to store user, organization, or application data.

Cloud storage services may be accessed through a cloud computer service, a web service application programming interface (API) or by applications that utilize the API.

7.5.1 Software as a Service (SaaS)

Very often the cloud storage providers also provide access to application software.

"Hosted software" differs from typical software in its installation and accessibility. Unlike most software, which is housed on the user's machine, hosted software related data processing and computing is performed on the remote host server. End users can access this data through a compatible Web browser.

Generally, hosted software is provided as a service to end users, who are billed monthly on pay-per-use or per-license fee billing method. Because all programs are installed at a provider's location, they are managed, upgraded and patched by the provider, ensuring that users always have access to updated, bug-free versions of the software they use.

7.6 Questions

7.6.1 Completion

7.0 **Computer data storage**, often called **storage** or **memory**, is a technology consisting of computer components and recording media used to retain _____ data

7.0 In practice, almost all computers use a storage_____, which puts fast but expensive (and small) storage options close to the CPU and slower but larger and cheaper options farther away.

7.0 _____ storage does not lose the data when the device is powered down—it is _non-volatile_

7.1 A **hard disk drive** is a data storage device used for storing and retrieving digital information using one or more rigid ("hard") rapidly rotating disks (platters) coated with _____ material

7.2 With _____ storage, data is recorded by making marks in a pattern that can be read back with the aid of light, usually a beam of laser light

7.2 The three most common optical media are CD, DVD and _____

7.3 A flash drive is a data storage device that includes flash memory with an integrated _____ interface

7.4.1 _____ disks, initially as 8-inch (200 mm) media and later in 5¼-inch (133 mm) and 3½-inch (90 mm) sizes, were a very widely used form of data storage and exchange from the mid-1970s into the late 2000s

7.4.3 Paper tape was widely used during much of the twentieth century for _____ communication

7.4.5 The **Zip drive** is a medium-to-high-capacity (at the time of its release) removable floppy disk storage system that was introduced by _____ in late 1994.

7.4.5 The _____ **drive** is a medium-to-high-capacity (at the time of its release) removable floppy disk storage system that was introduced by Iomega in late 1994

7.5 Some organizations have begun offering to rent storage to subscribers. This is referred to as "_____ storage"

7.6.2 Multiple Choice

7.0 Modern computer systems typically have_____
   a) two orders of magnitude more secondary storage than primary storage but data are kept for a longer time in primary storage
   b) two orders of magnitude more secondary storage than primary storage and data are kept for a longer time in secondary storage
   c) two orders of magnitude more primary storage than secondary storage and data are kept for a longer time in primary storage
   d) two orders of magnitude more primary storage than secondary storage but data are kept for a longer time in secondary storage
   e) none of the above

7.1 The time taken to access a given byte of information stored on a hard disk is typically a few thousandths of a second, or _____
   a) nanoseconds
   b) microseconds
   c) milliseconds
   d) picoseconds
   e) none of the above

7.1 The most common form factor for modern HDDs in desktop computers is _____ inches
   a) 8
   b) 5.25
   c) 3.5
   d) 2.5
   e) none of the above

7.1 The most common form factor for modern HDDs in laptop computers is _____ inches
   a) 8
   b) 5.25
   c) 3.5
   d) 2.5
   e)

7.1.1 A RAID system can provide the advantage of:
   a) lower price
   b) greater reliability
   c) faster upload speed
   d) all of the above
   e) none of the above

7.2 CD's hold about _____ of data
    a) 700 MB
    b) 4.7 GB
    c) 25 GB
    d) 50 GB
    e) none of the above

7.2 DVD's hold about _____ of data
    a) 700 MB
    b) 4.7 GB
    c) 25 GB
    d) 50 GB
    e) none of the above

7.2 Backups of large hard drives are now_____
    a) often made on external hard drives. Magnetic tapes are also used.
    b) often made on magnetic tape. External hard drives are used occasionally, but are too expensive for most installations
    c) usually made on magnetic tape or DVD's
    d) almost always made on DVD's
    e) none of the above

7.3 USB flash drives are often used for.
    a) storage
    b) data back-up
    c) transfer of computer files
    d) all of the above
    e) none of the above

7.3 USB flash drives are _____ than floppy disks
    a) more durable and more reliable
    b) less durable but more reliable
    c) more durable but less reliable
    d) less durable and less reliable
    e) none of the above

7.4 A **floppy disk** is a type of disk storage composed of a disk of thin and flexible _____ storage medium, sealed in a rectangular plastic enclosure
    a) optical
    b) magnetic
    c) semiconductor
    d) any of the above
    e) none of the above

7.4.2 Magnetic tape remains a viable alternative to disk in some situations due to
   a) lower cost per bit
   b) faster data access
   c) greater storage density
   d) all of the above
   e) none of the above

7.4.2 _____ have/has historically offered enough advantage in cost over disk storage to make it a viable product, particularly for backup, where media removability is necessary
   a) Punched cards
   b) Punched paper tape
   c) Magnetic tape
   d) all of the above
   e) none of the above

7.4.3 It was common to find a selection of _____ containing useful programs in most minicomputer installations
   a) Punched cards
   b) Punched paper tape
   c) Magnetic tape
   d) all of the above
   e) none of the above

7.4.5 The _____ format became the most popular of the superfloppy products which filled a niche in the late 1990s portable storage market
   a) CD
   b) cloud
   c) ZIP
   d) RAID
   e) none of the above

7.6.3 True-False

7. In practice, almost all computers use a storage hierarchy, which puts fast but expensive (and small) storage options close to the CPU and larger and more expensive options farther away

7. Generally, the fast but volatile technologies (which lose data when off power) are referred to as "memory", while slower persistent technologies are referred to as "storage"

7.1 Hard disks are typically about a million times faster than memory

7.1 Most HDDs in the early 1980s were sold to PC end users as an external, add-on subsystem

7.1.1. In a RAID system, data can be distributed across the drives in one of several ways, referred to as RAID levels

7.3 USB flash drives are immune to electromagnetic interference (unlike floppy disks), and are unharmed by surface scratches (unlike CDs).

7.4.4 By 1950 punched cards had been replaced by magnetic tape throughout almost all industry and government

8 Networks, Internet and the World Wide Web

One of the major reasons for the widespread popularity of personal computers has been the Internet and, in particular, the World Wide Web. These have allowed the computer to be used as a communications device, as well as a computation device. People have come to rely on these computation/communications devices for a wide range of *services*.

8.1 Internet

8.1.1 What is the Internet?

The Internet is a worldwide collection of networks. (Thus its name which is derived from the combination *inter-networking*).

The Internet links millions of businesses, government agencies, educational institutions, as well as individuals.

The Internet was originally developed by the US federal government, a project of **DARPA**. (*Defense Advanced Research Projects Agency*)

The original Internet project had two primary goals:

to help people working on government projects to communicate more easily and efficiently;

to create a robust communications system that would continue functioning even in even of national disaster (such as nuclear war.)

The Internet first came into being in 1964 as an interconnection between four *servers*: one at University of California Santa Barbara, one at University of California Los Angeles, one at Stanford University and one at the University of Utah.

It has since expanded to a system having 7.2 billion users (as of 2014[7].)

8.1.2 Internet Architecture

The *architecture* of the Internet is based on the specification of the *TCP/IP* protocol, and was designed to connect *any* two networks, even those which may be very different in internal hardware, software, and technical design.

Once two networks are interconnected, communication with TCP/IP is enabled end-to-end, so that any node on the Internet has the ability to communicate with any other node, no matter where they are.

This openness of design has enabled the Internet architecture to grow to a global scale.

---

[7] Numbers more recent than 2014 are difficult to obtain because of the expansion of the dark web.

In practice, an individual will often access the Internet from his home, using a *modem* to connect to a local *Internet service provider* (**ISP**).

The ISP connects to a regional network which, in turn, connects to a national network.

In an office, a computer (often a desktop computer) might be connected to a local area network and the company would have a corporate *intranet*, which, in turn, might connect to any of several national Internet service providers.

In general, small local Internet service providers connect to medium-sized regional networks which connect to large national networks, which then connect to very large bandwidth[8] networks which make up what is called the Internet *backbone*.

Most ISP's have several redundant network cross-connections to other providers in order to ensure continuous availability.

The companies running the Internet backbone operate very high bandwidth networks relied on by governments, corporations, large organizations, and other Internet service providers. Their physical infrastructures often include global connections through underwater cables and satellite links. These connections enable communication between different countries and continents.

8.1.3 Internet Services

One of the reasons that the Internet has had such a profound effect is that it provides a number of valuable "*services*" for its users.

Among these services are e-mail, file transfer protocol (FTP), instant messaging (IM), voice over internet protocol (VoIP), Chat Rooms, and (probably most widely known) the *World Wide Web* (WWW)

8.1.3.1 Internet Services: World Wide Web (WWW)

The **World Wide Web** is a system of "*web pages*" (documents and other web resources) which are identified by "*URL*'s" and are interlinked by "*hypertext links*".

---

[8]   The term *bandwidth* is often used to describe the amount of data transferred to or from the website or server within a prescribed period of time. It is usually described as a number of *bits per second*. This usage is technically incorrect, but *very* common.

The web pages can be accessed via the Internet using a program called a *"Web Browser"* (usually just called a **browser**)

The World Wide Web was designed and built by English scientist Tim Berners-Lee in 1989. He wrote the first web browser in 1990 while employed at CERN

> (*"Conseil Européen pour la Recherche Nucléaire"*; a European research organization based in Geneva, Switzerland, established in 1954, that operates the largest particle physics laboratory in the world.)

The public use of the Internet, and the World Wide Web in particular, began to explode in the early 1990's. This was sparked primarily by the 1993 release of *"Mosaic"*, the first widely available browser with graphic capabilities.

> Mosaic was developed by a team lead by Marc Andreeson working at the University of Illinois.

> Later Andreeson and his team formed a company which produced and marketed the browser *Netscape Navigator* (1994).

> In 1995, Microsoft released *its* browser, *Internet Explorer*. Explorer (mostly by virtue of being free) quickly became the most widely used browser in the world (attaining a 95% usage share in 2002.)

> > Explorer's usage share has since declined, with the launch of Firefox (2004) and Google Chrome (2008), as well as with the growing popularity of operating systems (such as OS X, Linux, iOS and Android) that do not support Internet Explorer

8.1.3.1.1 Difference between Internet and WWW

WWW is so widely and commonly used that many people fail to understand that there is more to the Internet and that WWW is, in fact, only one of many services provided by the Internet.

8.1.3.1.2 WWW and *Hypertext* concept

Hypertext is the underlying concept defining the structure of the World Wide Web.

> **Hypertext** is text displayed on a computer display or other electronic devices which contains references (*hyperlinks*) to other Web elements, either on the same or on a different Web page, which the reader can immediately access. The hypertext pages are interconnected by these *hyperlinks* which are typically activated by a mouse click, keypress sequence or by touching the screen.

> > In addition to *text*, hypertext is also used to implement links to tables, images, videos, sounds (music) and other content forms.

131

WWW pages are often written in the *Hypertext Markup Language* (***HTML***) which enables an easy-to-use and flexible connection and sharing of information over the Internet

8.1.3.1.2.1 HTML, Multimedia and Smartphones

The first browsers could only display text, but the release of graphic browsers, beginning with *Mosaic*, opened the door for multimedia Web sites and interactive Web pages.

HTML programs control the way browsers display text and images on computer screens. They also control the display of videos and sound (multimedia) and provide means for users to interact with the pages (entering text, checking boxes, selecting sections text or other objects…)

The introduction of smartphones brought about a significant change in the way many Web pages had to be designed. Cell phones have MUCH smaller displays than does a typical computer (4 to 5 inches for a phone compared to 14 to 15 inches for a relatively small laptop computer.) As a consequence, displays on the phones are much smaller than displays on computers. An image that would take up only a small part of the computer screen will either use almost all of the smart phone display, or will be displayed in a size so small that many details will not be visible. The amount of text that can be shown on a phone at any time will also be greatly reduced, unless the text is displayed in a size so small as to be illegible. Webpages designed to be displayed on large computer screens do not display well on small cellphone screens. Special browsers (microbrowsers) have been created to display webpages on smartphone screens and many websites provide alternative versions of their pages designed for small screens.

8.1.3.1.3 Web Servers

The function of a *web server* is to store and deliver *web pages* to clients.

The communication between client and server takes place using the Hypertext Transfer Protocol (HTTP).

The Web Pages delivered are most frequently HTML documents. HTML documents may include images, style sheets and scripts in addition to text content.

Many web servers also support server-side scripting using Active Server Pages (ASP), PHP, or other scripting languages. Usually, this function is used to generate HTML documents dynamically ("on-the-fly".) It is frequently used to access data in a database.

8.1.3.2 Internet Services: E-Mail

Electronic mail, (most commonly called **email** or **e-mail**), is a method of exchanging digital messages from a sender to one or more recipients. Email was the first service implemented on the Internet

Today's email systems are based on a *store-and-forward* model.

Email servers accept, forward, deliver, and store messages. The senders and receivers are not required to be online simultaneously. They connect by means of a *mail server*. The senders' messages are stored on the mail server until the receivers log on to download them.

Electronic mail predates the inception of the Internet and was in fact a crucial motivation for creating it.

The history of modern, global Internet email services reaches back to the early ARPANET.

Standards for encoding email messages were proposed as early as 1973.

It costs very little to send an email message, and many people have taken advantage of this to send numerous unsolicited messages, often advertising products or promoting get rich quick schemes. Such unsolicited email is often referred to as "spam".

8.1.3.3 Internet Services: FTP

Although e-mail is convenient for direct communications between users, it quickly became obvious that a different system was needed for transferring larger data files (such as computer programs, graphic images, audio files, ...)

The **File Transfer Protocol** (**FTP**) is a standard network protocol used to transfer computer files from one host to another host over a TCP-based network (such as the Internet.)

8.1.3.4 Internet Services: IM

Instant messaging (**IM**) is a type of online chat which offers real-time text transmission over the Internet.

Short messages are typically transmitted bi-directionally between two parties, when each user chooses to complete a thought and selects "send".

8.1.3.5 Internet Services: VoIP

Voice over IP (VoIP) is a methodology for the delivery of voice communications (and other kinds of multimedia sessions) over the Internet

using *Internet Protocol* (IP)

Other terms commonly associated with VoIP are **IP telephony**, **Internet telephony**, **broadband telephony**, and **broadband phone service**.

There are a number of VoIP services available. Probably the most widely recognized is Skype.

8.1.3.6 Internet Services: Chat Rooms

The term **chat room**, (or **chatroom**) is primarily used to describe real time conferencing that usually permits intercommunications among groups of users.

The primary use of a chat room is to share information via text with a group of other users.

Generally speaking, it is the ability to converse with multiple people in the same conversation that distinguishes chat rooms from instant messaging which is more typically designed for one-to-one communication.

New technology has enabled the use of file sharing and webcams to be included in some chat programs.

The users in a particular chat room are often connected by a common interest and chat rooms exist for a wide range of subjects.

8.1.4 AOL

AOL (*America OnLine*) was one of the early pioneers of the Internet in the mid-1990s, and the most recognized brand on the web in the United States. It would be difficult to underestimate the influence of AOL for the development of the Internet. (At one point over 50% of the CD's purchased in the world had an AOL logo.)

AOL originally provided a dial-up service to millions of Americans, as well as providing a web portal, e-mail, instant messaging and later a web browser (following its purchase of Netscape.) In 2001, at the height of its popularity, it purchased the media conglomerate Time Warner in the largest merger in U.S. history. AOL rapidly declined thereafter, partly due to the decline of dial-up and rise of broadband.

8.2 E-Commerce

The term **E-commerce** (also written as *e-Commerce*, *eCommerce* or similar variations), refers to trading in products or services using computer networks, such as the Internet.

When done properly, ecommerce is often faster, cheaper and more convenient than the traditional methods of buying and selling goods and services.

E-commerce is usually divided into three classifications: *Business-to-Consumer (B2C)*, *Consumer-to-Consumer (C2C)* and *Business-to-Business (B2B)*.

8.2.1 Business-to-Consumer (B2C)

B2C refers to transactions in which a consumer (user) purchases goods or services from a business.

Amazon.com is currently the largest company specializing in online B2C business.

8.2.1.1 Online shopping

Online shopping (sometimes known as **e-tail** from "electronic retail" or **e-shopping**) is a form of electronic commerce which allows consumers to buy goods or services from a seller over the Internet using a web browser. (Alternative names are: *e-web-store, e-shop, e-store, Internet shop, web-shop, web-store, online store, online storefront and virtual store.*)

An online shop evokes the physical analogy of buying products or services at a *bricks-and-mortar* retailer or shopping center.

Even to the point of providing an electronic "*shopping cart*" to allow users to select several items to purchase before paying for their entire selection.

8.2.2 Consumer-to-Consumer (C2C)

C2C refers to transactions in which one individual (a consumer) purchases goods and or services from another individual (not a company)

eBay Inc. is a multinational corporation and e-commerce company, providing consumer to consumer (as well as business to consumer) sales services via Internet.

8.2.3 Business–to-Business (B2B)

Business to Business or B2B refers to electronic commerce between businesses rather than between a business and consumers. B2B businesses often deal with hundreds or even thousands of other businesses, either as customers or suppliers. Carrying out these transactions electronically provides vast competitive advantages over traditional methods.

The number of B2B e-commerce transactions is much greater than the number of B2C and C2C transactions.

8.2.4. Electronic Transfer as a Form of Payment

The development of widespread e-commerce is supported by the parallel development of electronic means for transferring *value* on computer networks, especially on the Internet. Larger businesses (and banks in particular) have long made many of their payments by electronic wire transfer, but the virtually universal availability of electronic communication has brought this capability down to the level of the individual consumer. This includes, (but is not restricted to), the use of credit and/or debit cards for making payments. In fact, in the US, generally only the smallest transactions are paid in cash, and the society seems to be evolving towards a cashless economy.

As of 2014, most Americans carried less than $50 in cash in their wallets and half carry less than $20. In 2016, Mastercard found that, in the UK, the average person carried less than £5. By 2020, more than two-thirds of proximity mobile payments will be for items costing between $20 and $100, meaning consumers are becoming more comfortable making significant purchases with their mobile device -- not just the occasional $5 coffee.[9]

With the widespread acceptance of payment by electronic transfer has come the development of purely digital currencies.

8.2.4.1   Digital currency

Digital currency (digital money, electronic money or **electronic currency**) is a type of currency available only in digital form, not in physical form. It can be used for payments, just as physical currencies, but allows for instantaneous transactions and borderless transfer-of-ownership. Digital currencies include virtual currencies and cryptocurrencies as well as some central bank issued "digital base monies".

Like traditional money, these currencies may be used to buy physical goods and services, but may also be restricted to certain communities such as for use inside an online game or social network

8.2.4.2   Cryptocurrencies

Cryptocurrencies are a kind of (alternative) digital currency. Cryptocurrencies use decentralized control as opposed to centralized electronic money and central banking systems. The decentralized control of each cryptocurrency works through distributed ledger technology, (typically a blockchain[10]) that serves as a public financial transaction database.

Bitcoin, first released as open-source software in 2009, is generally considered the first decentralized cryptocurrency.

Since the release of Bitcoin, over 4,000 *altcoins* (alternative variants of Bitcoin, or other cryptocurrencies) have been created. Cryptocurrencies are used primarily outside existing banking and governmental institutions and are exchanged over the Internet. As the popularity of and demand for online currencies has increased,

---

[9]   www.forbes.com/sites/forbesfinancecouncil/2017/10/24/

[10] A blockchain is a continuously growing list of records, called *blocks*, which are linked and secured using cryptography. Each block typically contains a pointer as a link to a previous block, a timestamp and transaction data. By design, blockchains are inherently resistant to modification of the data.

so have concerns that such an unregulated person-to-person global economy may become a threat to society. Concerns abound that altcoins may become tools for anonymous web criminals.

Cryptocurrency networks display a lack of regulation that has been criticized as enabling criminals who seek to evade taxes and launder money.

Transactions that occur through the use and exchange of these altcoins are independent from formal banking systems, and therefore can make tax evasion simpler for individuals. Since charting taxable income is based upon what a recipient reports to the revenue service, it becomes extremely difficult to account for transactions made using existing cryptocurrencies

Systems of anonymity that most cryptocurrencies offer can also serve as a simpler means to launder money. Rather than laundering money through an intricate net of financial actors and offshore bank accounts, laundering money through altcoins can be achieved through anonymous transactions.

8.3 Wikis

A **wiki** is a website which allows collaborative modification of its content and structure. The encyclopedia project *Wikipedia* is by far the most popular wiki-based website, and is, in fact, one of the most widely-viewed sites of any kind of the world.

Wikis are generally designed with the philosophy of making it easy to correct mistakes, rather than avoiding mistakes in the first place.

Critics of publicly editable wiki systems argue that these systems could be easily tampered with, while proponents argue that the community of users can catch malicious content and correct it quickly.

8.4 Blogs

A **blog** (a truncation of the expression *weblog*) is a discussion or informational site published on the World Wide Web and consisting of entries ("posts") typically displayed in reverse chronological order (the most recent post appears first). The term "blogosphere" is commonly used to refer to the collection of all blogs together as a connected community.

Until 2009, blogs were usually the work of single individuals, and often covered single subjects.

More recently "multi-author blogs" (MAB's) have developed These typically have posts written by large numbers of authors but are professionally edited.

The emergence and growth of blogs in the late 1990s coincided with the advent of web publishing tools that facilitated the posting of content by non-technical users. Before this, creating and posting on a blog required some sophistication on the use of the Internet, and most blogs tended to emphasize technical and computer oriented themes.

A majority of blogs are interactive, allowing visitors to leave comments and even message each other on the blogs. In this sense, blogging can be seen as a form of social networking service.

Many bloggers report some sort of income from their blogs, most often in the form of ad revenue, but paid speaking engagements are also common.

8.5 Podcasts and Webcasts

A **podcast** is a form of digital media that consists of a series of audio or digital radio episodes, subscribed to and downloaded through web syndication or streamed online to a computer or mobile device. The word is made by combining "pod" and "broadcast.

A **webcast** is a media presentation distributed over the Internet using streaming media technology to distribute a single content source to many simultaneous listeners/viewers. A webcast may either be distributed live or on demand. Essentially, webcasting is "broadcasting" over the Internet

*Web*casting differs from *pod*casting in that webcasting refers to live streaming while podcasting simply refers to media files being made available on the Internet

8.6 Surfing the Web

Viewing a web page on the World Wide Web normally begins either by typing the *URL* of the page into a web browser, or by following a hyperlink to that page or resource. The web browser then initiates a series of background communication messages to fetch and display the requested page.

In the 1990s, using a browser to view web pages—and to move from one web page to another through hyperlinks—came to be known as '*web surfing*'

8.7 Using Search Engines

Since there are millions (billions?) of Web pages, nobody could possibly remember the URL's of all of them. For this reason, (and probably other reasons as well) programs known as *search engines* were developed to help users find documents that they might be interested in.

Search engines are programs that search for documents using specified *keywords*. They return lists of the documents where these keywords were found.

The term *search engine* really refers to a general class of programs, but the term is often used to specifically describe systems like *Google, Bing* and *Yahoo! Search*. Systems that enable users to search for documents on the World Wide Web

8.7.1 Spiders – Web Crawlers

Search engines are constantly updating their databases to keep their lists of documents current. They do this by using programs called ***spiders***, ***spiderbots*** or, often, ***web crawlers***. Web search engines get their information by *web crawling* from site to site. The "spider" checks for the standard filename *robots.txt*, addressed to it.

The robots.txt file contains directives for search spiders, telling it which pages to crawl. After checking for robots.txt and either finding it or not, the spider sends information back to be indexed, information such as the titles, page content, JavaScript, Cascading Style Sheets (CSS), headings, and/or information in an HTML meta tag. After a certain number of pages crawled, amount of data indexed, or time spent on the website, the spider will stop crawling and move on. No web crawler may actually crawl the entire reachable web.

8.8 Social Networking

A **social networking service** (also **social networking site** or **SNS**) is a platform to build social networks or social relations among people who share similar interests, activities, backgrounds or real-life connections.

Social network sites are web-based services that allow individuals to create a public profile, create a list of users with whom to share connections, and view and cross the connections within the system.

Most social network services are web-based and provide means for users to interact over the Internet.

Social network sites are varied and they incorporate new information and communication tools such as mobile connectivity, photo/video/sharing and blogging.

Online *community* services are sometimes considered a social network service, (though in a somewhat broader sense) the term *social network service* usually refers to an individual-centered service whereas online community services are group-centered.

Social networking sites allow users to share ideas, pictures, posts, activities, events, and interests with people in their network.

The main types of social networking services are those that contain category places (such as former school year or classmates), means to connect with friends (usually with self-description pages), and a recommendation system linked to trust.

Popular connection methods now combine many of these, with American-based services such as Facebook, Google+, LinkedIn, Instagram, Reddit, Pinterest, Vine, Tumblr, and Twitter widely used worldwide.

There are others outside of the US: Nexopia in Canada; Badoo, Bebo, Vkontakte (Russia), Delphi, Draugiem.lv (Latvia), iWiW (Hungary), Nasza-Klasa (Poland), Soup (Austria), Glocals in Switzerland, Skyrock, The Sphere, StudiVZ (Germany), Tagged, Tuenti (mostly in Spain), Myspace, Xanga and XING in parts of Europe; Hi5 in South America and Central America; Mxit in Africa;[9] Cyworld, Mixi, Renren, Friendster, Sina Weibo and Wretch in Asia and the Pacific Islands.

There have been attempts to standardize these services to avoid the need to duplicate entries of friends and interests (the *FOAF* standard and the *Open Source Initiative*).

A 2013 survey found that 73% of U.S adults use social networking sites.

8.9 How the Web Works

The functioning of the World Wide Web requires the support of many different structures, both physical and conceptual/intellectual.

8.9.1 HTML

HyperText Markup Language, commonly referred to as **HTML**, is the standard language used to create web pages. Web browsers can read HTML files and interpret them as code describing visible (and/or audible) web pages.

HTML is used to describe the structure of a website

HTML elements form the building blocks of all websites.

HTML allows images and objects to be embedded and can be used to create interactive forms.

It provides a means to create structured documents by denoting structural code for text, describing such things as headings, paragraphs, lists, links, quotes and other items.

8.9.2 Firewalls

In the late 1980's, people working in computer science became aware of the need for network security to protect the computers and data on their networks.

Worms and viruses were beginning to proliferate, and hackers were starting to attempt to gain access to the networks, some with purely malicious intent to damage the systems, and others hoping to gain access to the information stored in the system.

One of the security techniques that has been developed to protect networks is the *firewall*.

There are two kinds of firewalls: *network firewalls* and *host-based firewalls*.

A *network* **firewall** is a network security system that monitors and controls the incoming and outgoing network traffic based on predetermined security rules.

A network firewall typically establishes a barrier between one network and other outside networks.

Host-based firewalls provide software on a host that controls network traffic in and out of that single machine

8.9.3 Routers

Computers (on networks) must send and receive information to and from computers, often computers on other networks. It is the function of devices called **routers** to determine where to send and whether to accept/receive such information.

Typical home router

A **router** is a networking device that forwards *data packets* between computer networks. Routers perform the "traffic directing" functions on the Internet.

Information to be transmitted to other computers is divided into data packets.

Each data packet is typically forwarded from one router to another through the networks that constitute the internetwork until it reaches its destination node.

A *router* is connected to two or more data lines from different networks (as opposed to a *network switch*, which connects data lines from one single network).

When a data packet comes in on one of the lines, the router reads the address information in the packet to determine its ultimate destination. Then, using information in its routing table or routing policy, it directs the packet to the next network on its journey.

8.9.4 Servers

Recall from chapter 2, that:

A *server* is a computer that receives and responds to requests from client machines. The *server* provides *services* to *clients*, usually by sending information of some kind or receiving and processing information of some kind.

In context of the World Wide Web, a *server* is typically a computer (connected to the Internet, of course) on which a number of Web pages are stored, and which will send a copy of a page when it receives a request.

8.9.4.1 Dark Web

Most of the Web pages on the Internet are accessible by means of links in other pages and/or can be found using search engines. There are, however a large number of Web sites that are hidden from such searches. These "Darknet" websites are accessible only through specific encryption protected networks

Two examples of such networks are <u>Tor</u> ("The Onion Routing" project) and <u>I2P</u> ("Invisible Internet Project")

Tor browser and Tor-accessible sites are widely used among the darknet users and can be identified by the domain ".onion".

While Tor focuses on providing anonymous access to the Internet, I2P specializes on allowing anonymous hosting of websites.

Identities and locations of darknet users stay anonymous and cannot be tracked due to the layered encryption system. The darknet encryption technology routes users' data through a large number of intermediate servers. This protects the users' identity and guarantees anonymity. The transmitted information can be decrypted only by a subsequent node in the scheme, which leads to the exit node. The complicated system makes it almost impossible to reproduce the node path and decrypt the information layer by layer. Because of the high level of encryption, websites are not able to track geolocation and IP of their users, and users are not able to get this information about the hosts. Thus, communication between darknet users can talk, blog, and share files confidentially.

The darknet is often used for illegal activity such as illegal trade, and media exchange for pedophiles and terrorists.

8.9.5 TCP, UDP and IP

The **Transmission Control Protocol (TCP)** is a core protocol of the Internet.

It originated in the initial network implementation in which it worked together with the *Internet Protocol* (IP)

The combination is commonly referred to as *TCP/IP*.

TCP provides reliable, ordered, and error-checked delivery of a stream of packets between applications running on hosts communicating over an IP network.

TCP is the protocol used by major Internet applications such as the World Wide Web, email, remote administration and file transfer.

The **User Datagram Protocol (UDP)** is another widely used protocol of the internet.

UDP also provides delivery of a stream of packets between applications running on hosts communication over an IP network. The UDP packets, however, are not error checked. UDP is used for applications such as Internet telephony in which the time of arrival is important, and the loss or miscommunication of occasional packet can be tolerated.

8.9.6 Local Area Networks

As personal computers have become cheaper and easier to use, it is increasingly common for a family to have several computers in their home. These computers, then, are often connected to each other to facilitate intercommunication.

Such a group of interconnected computing devices forms what we call a *local area network* (LAN.)

Connecting the devices in a LAN allows the users to transfer information from one computer to another easily. It also allows them to share access to resources, such as printers and internet access devices.

In addition to computers and printers, LAN's often include such devices as routers, modems and gateways.

Devices in a LAN will typically communicate by means of either a physical medium (typically *twisted pair* cable) or radio waves (*WIFI*)

8.9.6.1 Intranet

The TCI/IP protocols can also be used for private local networks. Such networks are called intranets. Intranets can be connected to the Internet or can be completely isolated.

An intranet's websites and software applications look and act just like any others.

8.9.6.2 Extranet

If an intranet is connected to the Internet, its websites and software are typically protected by a firewall and are inaccessible from outside. When a company allows access to any part of its intranet (for example, some parts might be accessible to customers or suppliers outside the company) it is called an *extranet*.

8.9.6.3 [xcvi]Twisted Pair

Twisted pair cabling is a type of wiring in which two conductors of a single circuit are twisted together for the purposes of canceling out electromagnetic interference (EMI).

It was invented by Alexander Graham Bell.

Twisted Pair Cable

8.9.6.4 WIFI

Wi-Fi (or **WiFi**) is a local area wireless computer networking technology that allows electronic devices to connect to the network, mainly using the 2.4 gigahertz (12 cm) UHF and 5 gigahertz (6 cm) SHF ISM radio bands.

Many devices can use Wi-Fi, e.g. personal computers, video-game consoles, smartphones, digital cameras, tablet computers and digital audio players. These can use wireless technology to connect to other network resources such as printers, modems, routers, access points and/or gateways.

8.9.6.4.1 WIFI Encryption

Wireless networks are generally not as secure as wired networks. Wired networks, at their most basic level, send data between two devices which are connected by a network cable. Wireless networks, on the other hand, broadcast data in every direction to every device within a limited range that happens to be listening. Several wireless security protocols have been developed to protect the home wireless networks. These wireless security protocols include WEP, WPA, and WPA2.

In addition to preventing uninvited guests from connecting to your wireless network, wireless security protocols encrypt your private data as it is being transmitted over the airwaves.

8.9.7 Web Portals

Many Websites/Web Servers are configured as *Web Portals*.

A **web portal** is a specially designed **website** that brings information from diverse sources, like **emails, online forums** and (most frequently) **search engines**, together in a uniform way. Apart from this common search engines feature, web portals may offer other services such as e-mail, news, stock quotes, information from databases and even entertainment content. Portals provide a way for enterprises and organizations to provide a consistent "look and feel[11]" with access control and procedures for multiple applications and databases, which otherwise would have been different web entities at various URLs.

Examples of early public web portals were AOL and Yahoo.

8.10 Social Issues

Since the Internet is used in so many ways and by so many people, it has come to have important social effects.

New norms for Internet communications (netiquette) have had to be developed.

Information and communications systems have become targets for attempted theft and/or damage and this requires users to take special means to protect their systems.

---

[11] In software design, *look and feel* is a term used with respect to a GUI and comprises aspects of its design, including elements such as colors, shapes, layout, and typefaces (the "look"), as well as the behavior of dynamic elements such as buttons, boxes, and menus (the "feel"). The term can also refer to aspects of a non-graphical user interface (such as a command-line interface), as well – mostly to parts to its functional properties. The term is used in reference to both software and websites. Look and feel also applies to other products. In documentation, for example, it refers to the graphical layout (document size, color, font, etc.) and the writing style. In the context of equipment, it refers to consistency in controls and displays across a product line.

8.10.1 Netiquette/Ethics[12]

The term *"netiquette"* is used to refer to online etiquette over networks, such as online communities, forums, and even online learning environments.

Following the rules of netiquette improves the readability of your messages, lays the groundwork for making trustworthy connections and helps other people to better understand you

Here are a few guidelines to help you follow proper netiquette:

- **Stay on topic**. While discussion is encouraged, rambling conversations aren't conducive to a quality experience.

- **Use appropriate subject lines in your replies**. As a conversation evolves, it's helpful to change the subject line of a threaded message to reflect the changing topic. For example, if the subject line reads "Participation requirements" and the conversation evolves into a discussion on attendance, changing the subject line to "Attendance" in your reply would help others interested in the topic to join the conversation.

- **Avoid "I agree" and "Me, too!" messages**. Spending time reading messages without substance can be frustrating for all parties.

- **Avoid posting messages using all caps**. (IT'S LIKE SHOUTING!) It's OK to use all caps occasionally to emphasize a point, but you should only capitalize the individual words you want to highlight, not the entire sentence or paragraph.

- **Avoid writing errors, even when "talking" with one another**. Even though messages posted in the Main newsgroup are conversational and often informal; one should avoid posting messages with grammatical, spelling and typographical errors. Post intelligible messages despite the informality of the environment.

- **Carefully choose the format for your messages**. Long paragraphs are difficult for other people to follow on-screen. In general, try to limit each paragraph to five to seven lines and avoid using font styles, colors and sizes that are difficult to read. Please also avoid using stationery because it takes longer to download.

- **Be friendly**. Remember that even though you can't see the person you're connecting with online, you're still connecting with someone. Before posting a comment, ask yourself "Would I say this to a person face to face?" If the answer is "no," don't post it.

- **Avoid responding when emotions are running high**. If you're angry about something someone has posted, don't reply to their message until you've had a chance to calm down. Remember, your posted messages can be seen by everyone, even potential employers.

- **Before posting anyone's picture on any social networking site, get the person's permission.** Give your friends, family members and co-workers the opportunity to control their digital self.

---

[12] This section was *copied from the University of Phoenix Web Site*

8.10.1.1 Abbreviations and Acronyms

Abbreviations and acronyms are commonly used in online communications to quickly express words and phrases that we use in everyday conversation. Abbreviations and acronyms that are frequently used online include:

- BTW: By the way
- FYI: For your information
- IMO: In my opinion
- IMHO: In my humble opinion
- IMNSHO: In my not-so-humble opinion
- OIC: Oh, I see
- OTOH: On the other hand
- ROTFL: Rolling on the floor, laughing
- LOL: Laughing out loud
- TIA: Thanks, in advance
- <g>: Grin

8.10.1.2 Emoticons

Writers often use "emoticons" to convey their feelings in electronic communications like text messages, e-mails and message boards. Emoticons blend text and punctuation together to visually portray facial expressions.

Tilt your head slightly to the left to read the following emoticons:

- :-) Smiling
- ;-) Winking and smiling
- :-D Laughing
- :-(Frown
- :-o Oh!

8.10.1.3 Hashtags

A **hashtag** is a type of tag used on social networks allowing users to apply dynamic, user-generated tagging which makes it possible for others to easily find messages with a specific theme or content; it allows easy, informal markup.

Users create and use hashtags by placing the number sign or pound sign # (also known as the hash character) in front of a string of alphanumeric characters, usually a word or unspaced phrase, in or at the end of a message. The hashtag may contain letters, digits, and underscores Searching for that hashtag will yield each message that has been tagged with it.

The use of hashtags originated on Twitter but quickly spread to other social media, and later into the popular culture.

8.10.2 Computer Security

Computer security (also known as **cybersecurity** or **IT security**) is the protection of information systems from theft or damage to the hardware, the software, and to the information on them, as well as from disruption or misdirection of the services they provide.

Computer security includes controlling physical access to the hardware, as well as protecting against harm that may come through network access, data and code injection.

Also protecting against harm through malpractice by operators, whether intentional, accidental, or because they had been tricked into deviating from secure procedures.

The field of computer security is of growing importance due to the increasing reliance of computer systems in most societies.

Computer systems now include a very large range of portable devices,

including not only laptop computers, but also as a wide variety of "smart" devices,

including smartphones, televisions and tiny devices as part of the Internet of Things.

These are frequently easy targets for thieves.

Networks include not only *the* Internet and private data networks, but also Bluetooth, Wi-Fi and other wireless networks which are, in many cases, very public and easy to hack.

Computer security covers all the processes and mechanisms by which digital equipment, information and services are protected from unintended or unauthorized access, change or destruction and the process of applying security measures to ensure confidentiality, integrity, and availability of data both in transit and at rest.

8.10.2.1 Safe Surfing

The advancement and proliferation of technology has altered our lives in many ways.

Certain technologies, such as the Internet and email, have dramatically enhanced our ability to communicate and conduct business.

However, they also have their drawbacks.

Perhaps most alarming is that these technologies have made us vulnerable to a new realm of criminal activity.

147

The anonymity of the Internet, as well as the ability to search out victims quickly and effectively, has created incredible challenges for parents, educators and law enforcement who are on the front lines attempting to deter predators.

8.10.2.2 Malware

Malware, short for *malicious software*, is any software used to disrupt computer operations, gather sensitive information, or gain access to private computer systems.

Malware is defined by its malicious intent, acting against the requirements of the computer user.

It does not include software that causes *unintentional* harm due to some deficiency.

The term *badware* is sometimes used, and applied to, both true (malicious) malware and unintentionally harmful software.

Malware may be stealthy, intended to steal information or spy on computer users for an extended period without their knowledge, or it may be designed to cause harm, often as sabotage, or to extort payment.

'Malware' is an umbrella term used to refer to a variety of forms of hostile or intrusive software, including computer viruses, worms, Trojan horses, ransomware, spyware, adware, scareware, and other malicious programs. It can take the form of executable code, scripts, active content, and other software It is often disguised as, or embedded in, non-malicious files. As of 2011 the majority of active malware threats have been worms or Trojans rather than viruses.

8.10.2.2.1 Computer Viruses

A **computer virus** is a type of malicious software program ("malware") that, when executed, replicates by reproducing itself (copying its own source code) or infecting other computer programs by modifying them. Infected computer programs can also include data files, or the "boot" sector of the hard drive. When this replication succeeds, the affected areas are then said to be "infected" with a computer virus. The term "virus" is also commonly, but erroneously, used to refer to other types of malware. The defining characteristic of viruses is that they are self-replicating and install themselves without user consent.

8.10.2.2.2 Worms

A **computer worm** is a standalone malware computer program that replicates itself in order to spread to other computers. Often, it uses a computer network to spread itself, relying on security failures on the target computer to access it. Worms almost always cause at least some harm to the network, even if only by consuming bandwidth, whereas viruses almost always corrupt or modify files on a targeted computer.

Any code designed to do more than spread the worm is typically referred to as the "payload". Typical malicious payloads might delete files on a host system (e.g., the ExploreZip worm), encrypt files in a ransomware attack, or send out data such as confidential documents or passwords.

Probably the most common payload for worms is to install a *backdoor*[13]. This allows the computer to be remotely controlled by the worm author as a "zombie". Networks of such machines are often referred to as *botnets* and are very commonly used for a range of malicious purposes, including sending spam or performing DDoS[14] attacks.

8.10.2.2.3 Trojan Horses

In computing, **Trojan horse**, or **Trojan**, is any malicious computer program which is used to hack into a computer by misleading users of its true intent. The term is derived from the Ancient Greek story of the wooden horse that was used to help Greek troops invade the city of Troy by stealth. Although their payload can be anything, many modern forms act as a backdoor, contacting a controller which can then have unauthorized access to the affected computer. This infection allows an attacker to access users' personal information such as banking information, passwords, or personal identity (IP address) and/or download and install other malware, such as viruses or worms. Unlike computer viruses and worms, Trojans generally do not attempt to inject themselves into other files or otherwise propagate themselves. Due to the popularity of botnets among hackers and the availability of advertising services that permit authors to violate their users' privacy, Trojan horses are becoming more common. According to a survey conducted by BitDefender from January to June 2009, "Trojan-type malware is on the rise, accounting for 83-percent of the global malware detected in the world." Trojans have a relationship with worms, as they spread with the help given by worms and travel across the internet with them. BitDefender has stated that approximately 15% of computers are members of a botnet, usually recruited by a Trojan infection.

---

[13] A **backdoor** is a method, often secret, of bypassing normal authentication. Backdoors are often used for securing remote access to a computer.

[14] Denial of service is typically accomplished by flooding the targeted machine or resource with superfluous requests in an attempt to overload systems and prevent some or all legitimate requests from being fulfilled. In a **distributed denial-of-service attack (DDoS attack)**, the incoming traffic flooding the victim originates from many different sources. This effectively makes it impossible to stop the attack simply by blocking a single source.

8.10.2.2.4 Ransomware

Ransomware is computer malware that installs covertly on a victim's device (e.g., computer, smartphone, wearable device) and that either holds the victim's data hostage, or threatens to publish the victim's data, until a *ransom* is paid.

8.10.2.2.5 Spyware

Spyware is software that aims to gather information about a person or organization without their knowledge. The spyware may send such information to another entity without the consumer's consent,

Spyware is mostly used for the purposes of tracking and storing Internet users' movements on the Web and serving up pop-up ads to Internet users. When it is used for malicious purposes, however, its presence is typically hidden from the user and can be difficult to detect. Some spyware, such as keyloggers, may be installed by the owner of a shared, corporate, or public computer intentionally in order to monitor users.

8.10.2.2.6 Adware

Adware, or **advertising-supported software**, is any software package that automatically renders advertisements in order to generate revenue for its author. It often includes functions designed to analyze which Internet sites the user visits and to present advertising pertinent to the types of goods or services featured there.

The term is sometimes used to refer to software that displays *unwanted* advertisements and this would fall into the classification of malware.

In legitimate software, the advertising functions are integrated into or bundled with the program. Adware is usually seen by the developer as a way to recover development costs, and in some cases, it may allow the software to be provided to the user free of charge or at a reduced price. Some software is offered in both an advertising-supported mode and a paid, advertisement-free mode. The advertisement free mode is usually available by an online purchase of a license or registration code for the software that unlocks the mode, or the purchase and download of a separate version of the software

8.10.2.2.7 Scareware

Internet security writers use the term "scareware" to describe software products that produce frivolous and alarming warnings or threat notices. Usually these are for fictitious or useless commercial firewall and registry cleaner software. The software is often packaged with a look and feel that mimics legitimate security software in order to deceive consumers.

8.10.2.3 Cookies

Many people worry about "Cookies" as a security problem. Cookies are small files which are stored on a user's computer. They are designed to hold a modest amount of data specific to a particular client and website and can be accessed either by the web server or the client computer. A cookie allows information to be carried from one visit to the website (or related site) to the next without having to burden the server with massive amounts of data storage. Storing the data on the server without using cookies would also be problematic because it would be difficult to retrieve a particular user's information without requiring a login on each visit to the website.

Cookies do not in themselves present a threat to privacy, since they can only be used to store information that the user has volunteered or that the web server already has. Some commercial websites do include embedded advertising material which is served from a third-party site, and it is possible for such adverts to store a cookie for that third-party site. Such a cookie could contain information fed to it from the containing site - such information might include the name of the site, particular products being viewed, pages visited, etc. When the user later visits another site containing a similar embedded advert from the same third-party site, the advertiser will be able to read the cookie and use it to determine some information about the user's browsing history. This enables publishers to serve adverts targeted at a user's interests, so in theory having a greater chance of being relevant to the user. Many people see such 'tracking cookies' as an invasion of privacy since they allow an advertiser to build up profiles of users without their consent or knowledge.

8.10.3 Biometric Authentication

[15]Maintaining and managing access while protecting both the user's identity and the computer's data and systems has become increasingly difficult. Central to all security is the concept of authentication - verifying that the user is who he claims to be.

We can authenticate an identity in three ways: by something the user knows (such as a password or personal identification number), something the user has (a security token or smart card) or something the user is (a physical characteristic, such as a fingerprint, called a biometric).

Biometric authentication has been widely regarded as the most foolproof - or at least the hardest to forge or spoof. Since the early 1980s, systems of identification and authentication based on physical characteristics have been available to enterprise IT. These biometric systems were slow, intrusive and expensive.

---

[15]   Source www.computerworld.com/article/2556908/security0/biometric-authentication.html

Twenty years later, computers are much faster and cheaper than ever. This, plus new, inexpensive hardware, has increased interest in biometrics.

Because of its convenience and ease of use, fingerprint authentication has become the biometric technology of widest choice. A growing number of notebook PCs and computer peripherals are coming to market with built-in fingerprint readers. Scores of products are available, including keyboards, mice, external hard drives, USB flash drives and readers built into PC card and USB plug-in devices. Most of these units are relatively inexpensive.

8.10.4 Protection of Identity

Almost 50 million people subscribed to some form of identity-theft protection in 2010.

Those services, which cost about $120 to $300 a year, promise to protect your ID by monitoring your credit reports 24/7, scouring "black-market chat rooms" for your personal information, removing your name from marketing lists, and filing fraud alerts. Some throw in up to $1 million in insurance.

Many of these services come from banks, which account for more than half of the $3.5 billion a year spent on ID-theft protection subscriptions.

In a sense, consumers who buy this protection from their banks are, in fact, helping to foot the bill for services that financial institutions are obligated to provide. Federal law requires that they shield their customers from losses stemming from credit-card and bank-account fraud.

These protection plans provide questionable value, and some promoters of these services have been charged by the Federal Trade Commission for misleading sales practices and false claims.

This is not to say that Identity theft is not a serious problem.

In 2010 there were 8.1 million identity fraud victims (this was down 27% from the year before.) Clearly, this constitutes a serious threat, but the number, 8.1 million victims, overstates the danger.

According to the U.S. Department of Justice, more than 80 percent of what is being reported as identity theft involves fraudulent charges on existing accounts. In most of these cases a cardholder's liability is limited to $50 for a lost or stolen credit card and for debit cards, liability for an unauthorized transaction is limited to $50 if it's reported within two business days of the date a cardholder learns of it.

8.10.4.1 Social Engineering

Often identity theft (as well as many other types of breaches of security) is brought about by means of psychological manipulation, i.e. "social engineering"

This can take many forms. At its simplest, just a phone call asking for asking for information can often be all that is needed. More sophisticated schemes that have gained some public notoriety recently are "phishing" and "spear phishing".

8.10.4.1.1 Phishing

Phishing is a technique for obtaining private information by sending an e-mail that appears to come from a legitimate source—bank, credit card company, …—requesting "verification" of information and warning of some consequence if it is not provided. The e-mail will usually contain a link to a fraudulent web page that seems legitimate and has a form requesting information such as home address, ATM card's PIN number, and/or credit card number.

8.10.4.1.2 Spear Phishing

Phishing attempts directed at specific individuals or companies have been termed **spear phishing**. In contrast to bulk phishing, spear phishing attackers will gather and use personal information about their target to increase their probability of success. Spear phishing gained notoriety when it was learned that the tactic had been used successfully to gain access to accounts related to the 2016 presidential campaign of Hillary Clinton.

8.10.5 Some Other Social Concerns

8.10.5.1 Effects on Employment

Technological unemployment is the loss of jobs caused by technological change. Such change typically includes the introduction of labor-saving machines or more efficient processes, either of which permit the same work to be done by fewer people.

Historical examples include artisan weavers reduced to poverty after the introduction of mechanized looms.

A contemporary example of technological unemployment is the displacement of retail cashiers by self-service tills. In the case of the Internet, online shopping sites are reducing the number of "brick and mortar" stores, and eliminating many jobs for clerks, cashiers, etc.

That technological change can cause short-term job losses is widely accepted. The view that it can lead to lasting increases in unemployment has long been controversial.

Participants in the technological unemployment debates can be broadly divided into groups: optimists and pessimists.

Optimists agree that innovation may be disruptive to jobs in the short term, but assert that various compensation effects work to ensure there will not be a long term negative impact on jobs.

Pessimists, on the other hand, contend that, at least in some circumstances, new technologies can lead to a lasting decline in the total number of workers being employed.

The phrase "technological unemployment" was popularized by Lord Keynes in the 1930s, but the issue of machines displacing human labor has been discussed since at least Aristotle's time

The Internet has also created new methods for beginning new businesses. Many would be entrepreneurs are using the Internet to ask large numbers of people for small investments/donations to help provide capital to open a business. This practice is known as ***crowdfunding***.

kickstarter.com is the best known crowdfunding platform. The company's stated mission is to "help bring creative projects to life"

8.10.5.2 Effects on Education

The Internet has had a deep impact on the world of education. It has revolutionized the way education is imparted, the classrooms have been brought right in the homes of the students. There is little doubt that the Internet has become an engine of progress and has had an extremely invasive effect on our education. It has created a new fresh approach with online education.

The web technology has made it easy for students all over world to get skills they need to progress in society and enhance their life style. Students are becoming proficient with computers and the Internet at much younger ages. It motivates many students to acquire better thinking skills, remain well informed and grow as responsible citizens for their countries.

The vast majority of middle and high school teachers who are involved in high-level educational programs say the Internet has a "major impact" on their ability to access content and resources for their teaching.

8.10.5.2.1 Distance Education

On no area of education has the Internet had a greater effect than that of distance education.

Distance education or **long-distance learning** is the education of students who may not always be physically present at a school. Traditionally, this usually involved **correspondence courses** wherein the student communicated with the school via post. Today, the development of computerized communication has made **online education** not only possible, but, in fact quite common.

The widespread use of computers and the internet have made distance learning easier and faster, and today virtual schools and virtual universities deliver full curricula online. The capacity of Internet to support voice, video, text and immersion teaching methods made earlier distinct forms of telephone, radio, television, and text based education somewhat redundant. However, many of the techniques developed and lessons learned with earlier media are used in Internet delivery. In the United States in 2011, it was found that a third of all the students enrolled in postsecondary education had taken an accredited online course in a postsecondary institution

8.10.5.3 Net Neutrality

Net neutrality is the principle that Internet service providers should treat all data on the Internet equally, and not discriminate or charge differently by user, content, website, platform, application, type of attached equipment, or method of communication For instance, under these principles, internet service providers should not intentionally block, slow down or charge extra money for specific websites and/or online content. This is sometimes enforced through government mandate.

A widely cited example of a violation of net neutrality principles was the Internet service provider Comcast's secret slowing ("throttling") of uploads from peer-to-peer file sharing (P2P) applications (BitTorrent would be the best known example). Comcast did not stop blocking these protocols, until the Federal Communications Commission ordered them to stop.

AT&T was also caught limiting access to FaceTime, so that only those users who paid for AT&T's new shared data plans could access the application.

Supporters of net neutrality in the United States want to designate cable companies as common carriers, which would require them to allow Internet service providers (ISPs) free access to cable lines, the same model used for dial-up Internet. They want to ensure that cable companies cannot screen, interrupt or filter Internet content without a court order. Common carrier status would give the FCC the power to enforce net neutrality rules.

in April 2015, the FCC issued its Open Internet Order, which reclassified Internet access - previously classified as an information service - as a common carrier telecommunications service; i.e. a public utility. But on December 14, 2017, the Commission, voted to partially repeal the 2015 Open Internet Order, classifying Internet access once again as an information service.

8.11 Questions

8.11.1 Completion

8.1.1 The Internet was originally developed by the US federal government, a project of _____

8.1.1 The Internet first came into being in 1964 as an interconnection between four _____: one at University of California Santa Barbara, one at University of California Los Angeles, one at Stanford University and one at the University of Utah

8.1.2 In practice, an individual will often access the Internet from his home, using a(n) _____ to connect to a local *Internet service provider* (**ISP**)

8.1.3.1 The **World Wide Web** is a system of *"web*_____*"* (documents and other web resources)

8.1.3.1 WWW web pages are identified by _____'s

8.1.3.1 The public use of the Internet, and the World Wide Web in particular, began to explode in the early 1990's. This was sparked primarily by the 1993 release of "_____", the first widely available browser with graphic capabilities

8.1.3.1.2 WWW pages are often written in_____, which enables an easy-to-use and flexible connection and sharing of information over the Internet)

8.1.3.1.2 WWW web pages are interlinked by _____ links

8.1.3.1.3 The communication between client and server takes place using the Hypertext Transfer _____(HTTP).

8.2 The term **E-commerce** (also written as *e-Commerce, eCommerce* or similar variations), refers to trading in products or services using computer _____

8.2.1 _____.***com*** is currently the largest company specializing in online B2C business

8.2.2 _____***Inc.*** is an American multinational corporation and e-commerce company, providing consumer to consumer (as well as business to consumer) sales services via Internet.

8.3 A _____is a website which allows collaborative modification of its content and structure directly from the web browser

8.6 In the 1990s, using a browser to view web pages—and to move from one web page to another through_____—came to be known as '***web surfing***'

8.6 In the 1990s, using a browser to view web pages—and to move from one web page to another through hyperlinks—came to be known as '*web* _____,'

8.9.1 _____, is the standard language used to create web pages

8.9.2 A *network* _____is a network security system that monitors and controls the incoming and outgoing network traffic based on predetermined security rules

8.9.3 Computers (on networks) must send and receive information to and from computers, often computers on other networks. It is the function of devices called _____ to determine where to send and whether to accept/receive such information

8.9.4 A _____is a computer that receives and responds to requests from client machines

8.9.6 Devices in a LAN will typically communicate by means of either a physical medium (typically *twisted pair* cable) or radio waves (_____)

8.10.1 The term "_____" is used to refer to online etiquette over networks, such as online communities, forums, and even online learning environments

8.10.2.2 _____ is any software used to disrupt computer operations, gather sensitive information, or gain access to private computer systems.

8.10.4.1 kickstarter.com is the best known _____ platform

8.11.2 Multiple Choice

8.1.2 In general, small local Internet service providers connect to medium-sized regional networks which connect to large national networks, which then connect to very large bandwidth networks which make up what is called the Internet _____

a) architecture
b) backbone
c) infrastructure
d) Web
e) none of the above

8.1.3 The Internet has had a profound effect because it provides a number of valuable "*services*" for its users. Among these services is _____
a) FTP
b) IM
c) VoIP
d) all of the above are Internet services
e) none of the above

8.1.3.1 The **World Wide Web** is a system of "*web pages*" (documents and other web resources) which are identified by "_____" and are interlinked by *hypertext links*
a) URL's
b) VDT's
c) widgets
d) podlets
e) none of the above

8.1.3.1 Web pages can be accessed via the Internet using a program called a "*Web*
_____
a) Accesser
b) Searcher
c) Browser
d) Surfer
e) none of the above

8.1.3.1 The World Wide Web was designed and built by
a) Tim Berners-Lee
b) Marc Andreeson
c) Bill Gates
d) Steve Jobs
e) none of the above

8.1.3.1 Mosaic was developed by a team led by
a) Tim Berners-Lee
b) Marc Andreeson
c) Bill Gates
d) Steve Jobs
e) none of the above

8.1.3.1 Netscape Navigator was developed by a team led by
a) Tim Berners-Lee
b) Marc Andreeson
c) Bill Gates
d) Steve Jobs
e) none of the above

8.1.3.2 _____was the first service implemented on the Internet
a) WWW
b) FTP
c) Email
d) VoIP
e) none of the above

8.1.3.3 _____ is a standard network protocol used to transfer computer files from one host to another host over a TCP-based network (such as the Internet.)
a) WWW
b) FTP
c) Email
d) VoIP
e) none of the above

8.1.3.4 _____ is a type of online chat which offers real-time text transmission over the Internet
a) WWW
b) FTP
c) Email
d) VoIP
e) none of the above

8.1.3.5 _____ is a methodology for the delivery of voice communications (and other kinds of multimedia sessions) over the Internet
a) WWW
b) FTP
c) Email
d) VoIP
e) none of the above

8.2.1 _____ refers to transactions in which a user purchases goods or services from a company.
a) B2B
b) B2C
c) C2B
d) C2C
e) none of the above

8.2.2 _____ refers to transactions in which one individual purchases goods and or services from another individual.
a) B2B
b) B2C
c) C2B
d) C2C
e) none of the above

8.2.3 The number of _____ e-commerce transactions is much greater than the number of transactions of the other classes.
a) B2B
b) B2C
c) C2B
d) C2C
e) none of the above

8.7 Is a system that enables users to search for documents on the World Wide Web
a) *Google*
b) *Bing*
c) *Yahoo! Search*
d) all of the above
e) none of the above

8.8 Social network sites are web-based services that allow individuals to:
a) create public profiles
b) create lists of users with whom to share connections
c) view and cross the connections within the systems
d) all of the above
e) none of the above

8.9.3 A **router** is a networking device that forwards *data* _____ between computer networks
a) clusters
b) globules
c) packets
d) cells
e) none of the above

8.9.5 _____ is the protocol used by major Internet applications such as the World Wide Web, email, remote administration and file transfer
a) HTML
b) IP
c) TCP
d) all of the above
e) none of the above

8.10.1 Following the rules of netiquette _____
a) improves the readability of your messages
b) lays the groundwork for making trustworthy connections
c) helps other people to better understand you
d) all of the above
e) none of the above

8.10.4.1 Using the Internet to ask large numbers of people for small investments/donations to help provide capital to open a business is known as _____.

   a) kickstarting
   b) crowdfunding
   c) collaborating
   d) all of the above
   e) none of the above

8.11.3 True-False

8.1.2 The *architecture* of the Internet is based on the specification of the *TCP/IP* protocol, and was designed to connect *any* two networks

8.1.2 In order to reduce expenses, most ISP's limit their external Internet connections to one backbone connection.

8.1.3.1 In 1995, Microsoft released *its* browser, *Internet Explorer*. Explorer (mostly by virtue of being free) quickly became the most widely used browser in the world

8.1.3.1.1 The Internet is one of the services provided by WWW.

8.1.3.1.2 In addition to *text*, hypertext is also used to implement links to tables, images, videos, sounds (music) and other content forms

8.4 A majority of blogs are interactive

8.5 Webcasting differs from podcasting in that podcasting refers to live streaming while webcasting simply refers to media files placed on the Internet

9. Index

A

Abacus; 1
Accelerometer; 12, 49
Activity monitoring; 58
Address; 27, 72, 73
    Address Bus; 37, 73
    Addressable memory; 72
Adobe; 53, 111
Adware; 18
AI (artificial intelligence); 5
AIX; 45
ALU; 26, 71
Amiga; 46
Android; 43, 47, 47, 49
    Android Auto; 49
    Android TV; 49
    Android Wear; 49
Anti-virus; 18, 60
Antikythera mechanism; 1
AOL: 134, 144
Apple;8, 47, 49
    Apple II; 8
    Apple App Store; 48
    Apple Lisa; 46
    Apple Macintosh; 46
    Apple Newton; 10
    AppleDOS; 45
Application; 51
application programmer interface; 51
Application Software; 43, 51
Application suite; 51
Apps; 48
Artificial Intelligence; 5
ASR-33; 44
Astrolabe; 1
AT&T; 45
Atari; 46
ATM; 31
Audio output device; 32

B

Babbage; 3
Backdoor; 66

10-Answer Key

(Answers to *half* of the questions at ends of the chapters)

1.4 Questions:

1.4.1 Completion

1. Humans have always found it necessary to perform some kinds of calculations, and over the centuries, people have used many _____ to perform these calculations
   ANS: devices

   1.1.1 Several kinds of analog computers were constructed in ancient and medieval times to perform astronomical calculations. These include the Antikythera mechanism and the _____, both developed in ancient Greece (c. 150–100 BC)
   ANS: astrolabe

   1.1.4 In the United States, _____, the first general purpose, programmable computer was initially designed to compute artillery firing tables for the US army

   1.1.7.1 _____computers are computers used primarily by commercial and governmental organizations for critical applications and bulk data processing such as census, industry and consumer statistics, enterprise resource planning and transaction processing
   ANS: Mainframe

   1.1.7.2 The term *minicomputer* is no longer widely used. The term _____ *computer* is now preferred
   ANS: midrange

   1.1.7.3 Supercomputers were introduced in the 1960s, made initially, and for decades primarily by Seymour _____ at Control Data Corporation (CDC), then at subsequent companies, all bearing his name or monogram.
   ANS: Cray

   1.1.7.7 A(n) _____**computer** is a mobile computer with a touchscreen display, circuitry and battery in a single unit
   ANS: **tablet**

   1.1.8 With increased use of computers it became important to move data from one computer to another quickly and efficiently. This, then, motivated the development of computer _____
   ANS: networks

1.1.8.1 A(n) _____ is a computer that receives and responds to requests from client machines.
ANS: server

1.3.4 The term _____ was once used to describe a computer expert who used his technical knowledge to overcome a problem. It has come, in the popular culture, to be used to describe someone who uses his technical knowledge to break into computer systems.
ANS: hacker

1.4.2   Multiple Choice

1. The oldest known calculating device is the abacus which was invented in _____ over 2000 years ago.
   a) Asia
   b) Rome
   c) India
   d) Greece
   e) none of the above
   ANS: A

1.1.2 _____ described the binary number system that is used in all modern computers
   a) Pascal
   b) Leibnitz
   c) Newton
   d) Lovelace
   e) none of the above
   ANS: B

1.1.4 _____ was the world's first programmable, electronic, digital computer
   a) Colossus Mark 1
   b) ENIAC
   c) LEO 1
   d) UNIVAC
   e) none of the above
   ANS: A

1.1.5 It was in the _____ 's that IBM entered the computer business
   a) 1920
   b) 1930
   c) 1940
   d) 1950
   e) none of the above
   ANS: D

1.1.7.4 The first successfully mass marketed personal computer was the _____
   a) Apple II
   b) TRS-80
   c) Commodore PET
   d) IBM PC
   e) none of the above
   ANS: C

1.1.7.5 The _____ can be considered the first smartphone.
   a) Apple Newton
   b) IBM Simon
   c) Nokia Communicator
   d) Palm TX
   e) none of the above
   ANS: B

1.1.8.1 A _____ is a computer that receives and responds to requests from other machines
   a) client
   b) server
   c) peer
   d) all of the above
   e) none of the above
   ANS: B

1.4.3 True-False

1.1.3. One of the reasons that Babbage failed to make a working difference engine is that he turned his attention to a more advanced design which he called the *analytical engine*
   ANS: T

1.1.7.3 As of 2018, the fastest supercomputer was the Cray 1
   Ans   F,
   In Nov 2018, the IBM Summit at Oak Ridge National Laboratory became the fastest supercomputer in the world. Before Nov 2018, the two fastest machines were both in China.

1.1.7.8 The reduction in size, price and power consumption of computer components has made it possible to install general purpose computers as embedded systems in many devices)
   Ans   F
   The reduction in size, price and power consumption of computer components has made it possible to install **specialized** computers as embedded systems in many devices

1.3.4 The term **hacker** was once used to describe a computer expert who used his technical knowledge to overcome a problem. It has come, in the popular culture, to be used to describe someone who uses his technical knowledge to break into computer systems

Ans   T

1.3.5 Since the early 1980's computer crime and computer related crime have increased.

Ans   T

2.8   Questions:

2.8.1   Completion

2. The component which actually performs the actions/executes the commands that the computer carries out is called the processor or _____

Ans   CPU

2.2 The term "memory", (*primary* memory, primary storage) is _____ semiconductor memory, i.e. integrated circuits consisting of silicon-based transistors

Ans   addressable

2.2 Most home or office computers include magnetic disk drives and have only a minimal hardware initialization core and bootloader in ROM (known as the _____ in IBM-compatible computers).

Ans   BIOS

2.4 Traditional _____ devices include the keyboard, mouse and scanner.

Ans   input

2.4.4 A(n) _____ is a visual display which is sensitive to where a user is pressing on it and transmits this information to the computer

Ans   touchscreen

2.5.2.1.2 OLED's are used to produce _____ displays

Ans   flexible

2.5.2.3 The newest types of projectors are _____ projectors

Ans   handheld

2.8.2 Multiple Choice

2. Computer memory (Primary storage, Random access memory or RAM) is typically _____ (when the computer is turned off, the contents of memory are erased.)
   a) short term
   b) volatile
   c) temporary
   d) all of the above
   e) none of the above
   Ans   B

2. In most systems, the basic components will be mounted on or connected to the computer's _____
   a) motherboard
   b) CPU
   c) bay
   d) bus
   e) none of the above
   Ans   A

2.2 ROM is implemented using _____ types of memory
   a) expensive
   b) inexpensive
   c) volatile
   d) nonvolatile
   e) none of the above
   Ans   D

2.3 On modern computers _____ are normally used for secondary storage
   a) hard disk drives
   b) optical drives
   c) flash drives
   d) all of the above
   e) none of the above
   Ans   A

2.3 The time taken to access a given byte of information stored in random-access memory is measured in billionths of a second (_____.)
   a) microseconds
   b) milliseconds
   c) nanoseconds
   d) macroseconds
   e) none of the above
   Ans   C

2.5.2.1.1 Most of the modern flat-panel displays use _____ technologies
   a) CRT
   b) LCD
   c) VDT
   d) DVD
   e) none of the above
   Ans   B

2.6.4 An Ethernet port is an example of a(n) _____ device
   a) input
   b) output
   c) communications
   d) storage
   e) none of the above
   Ans   C

2.8.3   True-False

2. Almost all modern computers have pretty much the same design. They all have the same basic components
   Ans   T

2.2 Access to locations in RAM is generally much faster than to locations in ROM
   Ans   T
   Access to locations in RAM is generally much faster than to locations in ROM. It is for this reason that only minimal initialization software will be in ROM

2.3 Rotating *optical storage devices* (such as CD and DVD drives), have much shorter access times than do rotating magnetic storage devices, such as hard disks.
   Ans   F
   Rotating *optical storage devices* (such as CD and DVD drives), have even longer access times than do rotating magnetic storage devices, such as hard disks

2.4.5 Most laptops and tablets come with digital cameras built in.
   Ans   T

2.6.1 Early network interface controllers were commonly built into computer motherboards, but most on most modern computers, they are implemented on expansion cards that plugged into a computer bus
   Ans   F
   Early network interface controllers were commonly implemented on expansion cards that plugged into a computer bus, but most modern computers have a network interface built into the motherboard

3.4 Questions

3.4.1 Completion

3. _____ software is software which provides an interface and services both for users and for other software
Ans   System

3.1.1.4.2.2 On PCs, _____ is the most popular operating system
Ans   Windows

3.1.1.4.2.3 _____ has the largest installed base of all general-purpose operating systems
Ans   Linux

3.1.2 The term *system software* can also be used for software development tools (like_____, linkers and debuggers)
Ans   compilers

3.2 The collective noun **application software** refers to all *applications* collectively. This distinguishes it from _____ software, which is mainly involved with running the computer.
Ans   system

3.2 _____*Software* can refer to video games, screen savers, programs to display motion pictures or play recorded music
Ans   Entertainment

3.4.2 Multiple Choice

3. Computer programs (collectively known as *Computer Software*) can generally be divided into two classifications:
a) System Software and User Software
b) System Software and Application Software
c) Network Software and User Software
d) Network Software and Application Software
e) none of the above
Ans   B

3. _____ software is software designed to provide specific services for users
a) System
b) User
c) Network
d) Application
e) none of the above
Ans   D

3.1.1.3.1 The first successful multiuser time sharing system was
   a) DTSS
   b) UNIX
   c) Multics
   d) ENIAC
   e) none of the above
   Ans   A

3.1.1.4.1 _____ is a personal computer operating system with a command line interface.
   a) AppleDOS
   b) CP/M
   c) MS-DOS
   d) all of the above
   e) none of the above
   Ans   D

3.1.1.5.1 Android works with a user interface that is mainly based on direct manipulation, using touch gestures that loosely correspond to real-world actions, such as_____, to manipulate on-screen objects
   a) swiping
   b) tapping
   c) pinching
   d) all of the above
   e) none of the above
   Ans   D

3.4.3   True-False

3.1.1.2 In the early days of computing, CPU time was expensive, and peripherals were very slow
   Ans   T

3.1.1.4 Personal computers are intended to be operated directly by an end-user who is not necessarily a computer expert or technician
   Ans   T

3.1.1.5 The vast majority of modern smartphones use one of three operating systems: Android, Linux, or iOS
   Ans   F
   The vast majority of modern smartphones use one of *two* operating systems: Android or iOS

3.3.1.1 There are two contrasting ethical views on the issue of piracy, and both have their valid points.

Ans   T

3.3.1.2.2.1 The majority of identity theft victims do not realize that they are victims until it has negatively impacted their lives.

Ans   T

3.3.1.2.2.4 Computer viruses currently cause hundreds of thousands of dollars worth of economic damage each year.

Ans   F

Computer viruses currently cause billions of dollars' worth of economic damage each year

4.11   Questions

4.11.1   Completion

4. In a desktop computer, most of the electronic components are housed in an enclosure a called the _____unit

Ans   system

4.1.1 Most modern CPUs are _____ meaning they are contained on a single integrated circuit (IC) chip.

Ans   microprocessors

4..4 _____memory, is random access memory (RAM) that a computer microprocessor can access more quickly than it can access regular RAM

Ans   Cache

4.6.1.16 One of the earliest (and still one of the most commonly used) systems for storing representations of characters in computer memory is_____

Ans   ASCII

4.7.1 An *expansion bus* is a *computer bus* which moves information between the internal hardware of a computer system (including the CPU and RAM) and peripheral devices. It is a collection of wires and _____ that allows for the *expansion* of a computer

Ans   protocols

4.9.1 A **USB port** is a standard cable connection interface for personal computers and consumer electronics devices. USB stands for Universal Serial_____, an industry standard for short-distance digital data communications

Ans   Bus

4.11.2 Multiple Choice

4 In a desktop computer, most of the electronic components are housed in an enclosure a called the _____ .
   a) motherboard
   b) cache
   c) system unit
   d) all of the above
   e) none of the above
   Ans   C

4.1 The term *Motherboard* specifically refers to a(n) _____ with expansion capability
   a) PCB
   b) CPU
   c) ALU
   d) RAM
   e) none of the above
   Ans   A

4.1.1.2 One might describe the speed of a microprocessor as a number of _____
   a) Hertz
   b) MIPS
   c) FLOPS
   d) any of the above
   e) none of the above
   Ans   D

4.1.1.3 _____ is a CPU design strategy based on the insight that a simplified instruction set can provide higher performance. The simplified instruction set allows the CPU to be optimized to execute these instructions more efficiently
   a) FLOPS
   b) ROM
   c) RISC
   d) CISC
   e) none of the above
   Ans   C

4.3 An **instruction cycle** (sometimes called a **fetch–decode–execute cycle**) is the basic operational process of a computer. It is the process by which a computer retrieves a program instruction from its memory, determines what actions the instruction dictates, and carries out those actions. This cycle is repeated continuously by a computer's _____, from boot-up to when the computer is shut down.
a) ALU
b) Ports
c) motherboard
d) CPU
e) none of the above
Ans   D

4.5 The computer_____, locations in ROM
a) cannot read information from, and cannot write to
b) cannot read information from, but can write to
c) can read information from, but cannot write to
d) can read information from, and can write to
e) none of the above
Ans   C

4.6 The primary function of a computer is _____ *processing.*
a) information
b) numerical
c) binary
d) ASCII
e) none of the above
Ans   A

4.8 Drive bays are most commonly used to store _____, ,
a) disk drives
b) front-end USB ports
c) I/O bays
d) all of the above
e) none of the above
Ans   A

4.11.3 True-False

4.2.1 RAM is considered "random access" because it is hard to predict how long it will take for the processor to access any given cell.
Ans   F
RAM is considered "random access" because you can access any memory cell directly without accessing the previous cells first

4.5 ROM is implemented using *nonvolatile* types of memory

Ans   T

4.6.1.1 ASCII codes use 8 bits

Ans   F

Computer designers have come to use binary (two state) equipment to store representations of data

5.5   Questions

5.5.1   Completion

5. Examples of _____ devices include keyboards, mouse, scanners, digital cameras and joysticks

Ans   input

5.1 In computing, a **computer keyboard** is a(n) _____-style device which uses an arrangement of buttons or keys to act as electronic switches

Ans   typewriter

5.1.1.3 The vast majority of flexible keyboards in the market are made from

_____

Ans   silicone

5.1.2.1 The common _____-based layout was designed early in the era of mechanical typewriters, so its ergonomics were compromised to allow for the mechanical limitations of the typewriter

Ans   QWERTY

5.2 An *image* _____ is a device that optically scans images and converts them to digital representations of the images

Ans   scanner

5.4.2   Multiple Choice

5. A _____ is an example of an input device
   a) keyboard
   b) mouse
   c) scanner
   d) all of the above
   e) none of the above

Ans   D

5.1.1.1 There are three different PC keyboards: The three differ somewhat in the placement of:
a) the function keys
b) the control keys
c) the return key
d) all of the above
e) none of the above
Ans　　D

5.1.1.4 _____ keyboards have become very popular for cell phones, due to the additional cost and space requirements of other types of hardware keyboards
a) Projection
b) Flexible
c) Software
d) all of the above
e) none of the above
Ans　　C

5.1.2.3 The _____ keyboard layout is widely used in Germany and much of Central Europe
a) QWERTZ
b) DVORAK
c) AZERTY
d) QWERTY
e) none of the above
Ans　　A

5.2 An *image* scanner—usually abbreviated to just **scanner**—is a device that optically scans images and converts them to digital representations of the images. There are various kinds of scanners. Among them are:
_____scanners where the document is placed on a glass window for scanning
a) flatbed
b) window
c) document
d) industrial
e) none of the above
Ans　　A

5.3 A _____**device** is an input interface that allows a user to input spatial data to a computer by controlling the position of a cursor on the computer display
a) cursor
b) spatial
c) pointing
d) all of the above
e) none of the above
Ans　　C

5.3.1 The optical mouse _____
  a) is cheaper than a mechanical mouse and responds more slowly
  b) is cheaper than a mechanical mouse and responds more quickly
  c) is more expensive than a mechanical mouse and responds more slowly
  d) is more expensive than a mechanical mouse and responds more quickly
  e) none of the above
  Ans   D

5.3.4 A _____ touch screen panel is coated with a thin metallic electrically conductive and resistive layer that causes a change in the electrical current which is registered as a touch event
  a) resistive
  b) surface wave
  c) capacitive
  d) all of the above
  e) none of the above
  Ans   A

5.3.6 _____ are a common feature of laptop computers, and are also used as a substitute for a mouse where desk space is scarce
  a) Touchscreens
  b) Touchpads
  c) Joysticks
  d) all of the above
  e) none of the above
  Ans   B

5.4.3 True-False

5.1 A keyboard typically has characters engraved or printed on the keys and each press of a key typically corresponds to a single written symbol
  Ans   T

5.1.1.1 The IEEE has established a standard computer keyboard design that all manufacturers conform to.
  Ans   F
  There is no standard computer keyboard, although many manufacturers imitate the keyboards of PCs

5.2 There are a number of different arrangements of alphabetic, numeric, and punctuation symbols on keys of computer keyboards
  Ans   T

5.3.3 Most joysticks include buttons called *triggers*
  Ans   T

5.3.4 Capacitive touch screens are not affected by outside elements and have high clarity
  Ans   T

6.3 **Questions**

6.3.1 **Completion**

6. After a computer executed a program, has processed some data, it will probably be desirable for the computer to produce some kind of tangible effect in the outside world; for it to produce some kind of _____

Ans   output

6.1.1.2.2 A(n) _____ *display* consists of two glass plates separated by a thin gap filled with a gas such as neon

Ans   plasma

6.1.1.3 Flexible OLED's are often used in _____ devices

Ans   wearable

6.1.2.2 _____ printing differs from other printing technologies in that each page is always rendered in a single continuous process without any pausing in the middle, while other technologies like inkjet can pause every few lines.

Ans   Laser

6.1.2.4.5 _____ printers are widely used in cash registers, ATMs, gasoline dispensers and some older inexpensive fax machines.

Ans   Thermal

6.1.3.1 A(n) _____ is a small line attached to the end of a stroke in a letter or symbol.

Ans   serif

6.2 _____ are designed to allow a single user to listen to an audio source privately, in contrast to a speaker, which emits sound into the open air, for anyone nearby to hear.

Ans   Headphones

6.2 In the context of telecommunication, a _____ is a combination of a headphone and a microphone.

Ans   headset

6.3.2 Multiple Choice

6.1.1 A *VDU* is:
a) a monitor
b) a printer
c) a wearable
d) a speaker
e) none of the above
Ans A

6.1.1.3 Flexible OLED's, which are often used in *wearable* devices,
a) are relatively heavy and are somewhat power hungry
b) are light weight but are somewhat power hungry
c) are relatively heavy but require little power
d) are light weight and require little power
e none of the above
Ans D

6.1.2 _____ **printers** spray tiny dots of ink on a surface to create an image
a) inkspray
b) inkjet
c) inkdot
d) spraydot
e) none of the above
Ans B

6.1.2.3 _____ printing is a type of computer printing which uses a print head that prints by impact, striking an ink-soaked cloth ribbon against the paper
a) Dot matrix
b) Inkjet
c) Laser
d) Thermal
e) none of the above
Ans A

6.1.2.4.3 _____ printers are most commonly used as color office printers, and are excellent at printing on transparencies and other non-porous media
a) Dot matrix
b) Inkjet
c) Laser
d) Thermal
e) none of the above
Ans E
Solid ink

6.1.2.4.4 _____ printers are now increasingly used as dedicated consumer photo printers
a) Dot matrix
b) Inkjet
c) Laser
d) Thermal
e) none of the above
Ans   E
Dye sublimation

6.1.2.4.6 These printers were also referred to as *letter-quality printers* because they could produce text which was as clear and crisp as a typewriter.
a) dye-sub
b) daisy-wheel
c) dot-matrix
d) thermal
e) none of the above
Ans   B

6.3.3 True-False

6.1.1.2.2 Very large displays generally use ***plasma display technology***
Ans   T

6.1.1.2.2 Liquid crystal displays are lightweight, compact, portable and cheap and they are also more reliable than CRTs.
Ans   T

6.1.2.1 Consumer inkjet printers with photographic-quality printing are widely available
Ans   T

6.1.3.1 There is considerable debate as to which type of font, serif or sans-serif, is easier to read. There are studies to support both sides of the issue.
Ans   T

6.1.3.1 The text in this question is displayed using a *serif* font.
Ans   T

7.6 Questions

7.6.1 Completion

7.0 **Computer data storage**, often called **storage** or **memory**, is a technology consisting of computer components and recording media used to retain _____ data
Ans   digital

7.0 _____storage does not lose the data when the device is powered down—it is *non-volatile*

Ans   Secondary

7.2 With _____ storage, data is recorded by making marks in a pattern that can be read back with the aid of light, usually a beam of laser light

Ans   optical

7.3 A flash drive is a data storage device that includes flash memory with an integrated _____ interface

Ans   USB

7.4.3 Paper tape was widely used during much of the twentieth century for _____communication

Ans   teleprinter

7.4.5 The _____**drive** is a medium-to-high-capacity (at the time of its release) removable floppy disk storage system that was introduced by Iomega in late 1994

Ans   Zip

7.6.2   Multiple Choice

7.0 Modern computer systems typically have_____

a) two orders of magnitude more secondary storage than primary storage but data are kept for a longer time in primary storage

b) two orders of magnitude more secondary storage than primary storage and data are kept for a longer time in secondary storage

c) two orders of magnitude more primary storage than secondary storage and data are kept for a longer time in primary storage

d) two orders of magnitude more primary storage than secondary storage but data are kept for a longer time in secondary storage

e) none of the above

Ans   B

7.1 The most common form factor for modern HDDs in desktop computers is _____ inches

a) 8
b) 5.25
c) 3.5
d) 2.5
e) none of the above

Ans   C

7.1.1   A RAID system can provide the advantage of:
   a) lower price
   b) greater reliability
   c) faster upload speed
   d) all of the above
   e) none of the above
   Ans   D

7.2 DVD's hold about _____ of data
   a) 700 MB
   b) 4.7 GB
   c) 25 GB
   d) 50 GB
   e) none of the above
   Ans   B

7.3 USB flash drives are often used for.
   a) storage
   b) data back-up
   c) transfer of computer files
   d) all of the above
   e) none of the above
   Ans   A

7.4 A **floppy disk** is a type of disk storage composed of a disk of thin and flexible _____ storage medium, sealed in a rectangular plastic enclosure
   a) optical
   b) magnetic
   c) semiconductor
   d) any of the above
   e) none of the above
   Ans   B

7.4.2 _____ have/has historically offered enough advantage in cost over disk storage to make it a viable product, particularly for backup, where media removability is necessary
   a) Punched cards
   b) Punched paper tape
   c) Magnetic tape
   d) all of the above
   e) none of the above
   Ans   C

7.4.5 The _____ format became the most popular of the superfloppy products which filled a niche in the late 1990s portable storage market

a) CD
b) cloud
c) ZIP
d) RAID
e) none of the above

Ans   C

7.6.3 True-False

7. In practice, almost all computers use a storage hierarchy, which puts fast but expensive (and small) storage options close to the CPU and larger and more expensive options farther away

Ans   T

7.1 Hard disks are typically about a million times faster than memory

Ans   F

Hard disks are typically about a million times slower than memory

7.1.1. In a RAID system, data can be distributed across the drives in one of several ways, referred to as RAID levels

Ans   T

7.4.4 By 1950 punched cards had been replaced by magnetic tape throughout almost all industry and government

Ans   F

By 1950 punched cards had become ubiquitous in industry and government

8.11 Questions

8.11.1 Completion

8.1.1 The Internet was originally developed by the US federal government, a project of _____

Ans   DARPA

8.1.2 In practice, an individual will often access the Internet from his home, using a(n) _____ to connect to a local *Internet service provider* (**ISP**)

Ans   modem

8.1.3.1 WWW web pages are identified by _____'s

Ans   URL

8.1.3.1.2 WWW pages are often written in_____, which enables an easy-to-use and flexible connection and sharing of information over the Internet)

Ans   HTML

8.1.3.1.3 The communication between client and server takes place using the Hypertext Transfer _____(HTTP).

Ans   Protocol

8.2.1 _____.*com* is currently the largest company specializing in online B2C business

Ans   Amazon

8.3 A _____is a website which allows collaborative modification of its content and structure directly from the web browser.

Ans   wiki

8.6 In the 1990s, using a browser to view web pages—and to move from one web page to another through hyperlinks—came to be known as '*web* _____,

Ans   surfing

8.9.2 A *network* _____is a network security system that monitors and controls the incoming and outgoing network traffic based on predetermined security rules

Ans   firewall

8.9.4 A _____is a computer that receives and responds to requests from client machines

Ans   server

8.9.6 Devices in a LAN will typically communicate by means of either a physical medium (typically *twisted pair* cable) or radio waves (_____)

Ans   wifi

8.10.2.2 _____ is any software used to disrupt computer operations, gather sensitive information, or gain access to private computer systems.

Ans   malware

8.11.2 Multiple Choice

8.1.2 In general, small local Internet service providers connect to medium-sized regional networks which connect to large national networks, which then connect to very large bandwidth networks which make up what is called the Internet _____

a) architecture
b) backbone
c) infrastructure
d) Web
e) none of the above
Ans   B

8.1.3.1 The **World Wide Web** is a system of *"web pages"* (documents and other web resources) which are identified by "_____" and are interlinked by *hypertext links*
a) URL's
b) VDT's
c) widgets
d) podlets
e) none of the above
Ans   A

8.1.3.1 The World Wide Web was designed and built by
a) Tim Berners-Lee
b) Marc Andreeson
c) Bill Gates
d) Steve Jobs
e) none of the above
Ans   A

8.1.3.1 Netscape Navigator was developed by a team led by
a) Tim Berners-Lee
b) Marc Andreeson
c) Bill Gates
d) Steve Jobs
e) none of the above
Ans   B

8.1.3.3 _____ is a standard network protocol used to transfer computer files from one host to another host over a TCP-based network (such as the Internet.)
a) WWW
b) FTP
c) Email
d) VoIP
e) none of the above
Ans   B

8.1.3.5 _____ is a methodology for the delivery of voice communications (and other kinds of multimedia sessions) over the Internet
a) WWW
b) FTP
c) Email
d) VoIP
e) none of the above
Ans   D

8.2.2 _____ refers to transactions in which one individual purchases goods and or services from another individual.
a) B2B
b) B2C
c) C2B
d) C2C
e) none of the above
Ans   D

8.7 Is a system that enables users to search for documents on the World Wide Web
a) *Google*
b) *Bing*
c) *Yahoo! Search*
d) all of the above
e) none of the above
Ans   D

8.9.3 A **router** is a networking device that forwards *data* _____ between computer networks
a) clusters
b) globules
c) packets
d) cells
e) none of the above
Ans   C

8.10.1 Following the rules of netiquette _____
   a) improves the readability of your messages
   b) lays the groundwork for making trustworthy connections
   c) helps other people to better understand you
   d) all of the above
   e) none of the above
   Ans   D

8.11.3 True-False

8.1.2 The *architecture* of the Internet is based on the specification of the *TCP/IP* protocol, and was designed to connect *any* two networks
Ans   T8.1.2 In order to reduce expenses, most ISP's limit their external Internet connections to one backbone connection.
Ans   F
Most ISP's have several redundant network cross-connections to other providers in order to ensure continuous availability

8.1.3.1.1 The Internet is one of the services provided by WWW.
Ans   F
WWW is, in fact, only one of many services provided by the Interne

8.4 A majority of blogs are interactive
Ans   T

11-Image References

[i] Abacus: *This image comes from the 12th edition of the* Encyclopædia Britannica *or earlier. The copyrights for that book have expired and this image is in the **public domain***

[ii] *Pullan, J. M. (1968). The History of the Abacus. New York, NY: Frederick A. Praeger, Inc., Publishers. ISBN 978-0-09-089410-9. LCCN 72075113*

[iii] *Credit: Antikythera Mechanism Research Project*

[iv] Astrolabe: Photo taken by Andrew Dunn Whipple Museum of the History of Science Location Cambridge, United Kingdom Established 1944 Website, The Whipple Museum's website. Andrew Dunn uploaded it first to the English Wikipedia on 6. Nov. 2004 and released it there under CC-BY-SA-2.0

[v] Pascal's calculator: Photographer David Monniaux / (2005) Permission is granted to copy, distribute and/or modify this document under the terms of the **GNU Free Documentation License**, Version 1.2 or any later version published by the Free Software Foundation;

[vi] Leibnitz calculator: "Leibnitzrechenmaschine" by User:Kolossos - recorded by me in de:Technische Sammlungen der Stadt Dresden (with photo permission). Licensed under CC BY-SA 3.0 via Commons

[vii] Slide Rule: ArnoldReinhold - Own work (I took this picture of an artifact in my possession on February 3, 2006. The object itself is functional in nature, was created before 1970 and has no copyright notice, either on front or back.) Permission is granted to copy, distribute and/or modify this document under the terms of the **GNU Free Documentation License**, Version 1.2 or any later version published by the Free Software Foundation

[viii] Babbage Analytical Engine: Bruno Barral: licensed under the Creative Commons Attribution-Share Alike 2.5 Generic license

[ix] By Unknown - This file is from the collections of The National Archives (United Kingdom), catalogued under document record FO850/234. For high quality reproductions of any item from The National Archives collection please contact the image library.This tag does not indicate the copyright status of the attached work. A normal copyright tag is still required. See Commons:Licensing for more information.English | français | italiano | македонски | +/−, Public Domain, https://commons.wikimedia.org/w/index.php?curid=501979

[x] ENIAC: US Army Photo: This image is a work of a U.S. Army soldier or employee, taken or made as part of that person's official duties. As a work of the U.S. federal government, the image is in the public domain

[xi] UNIVAC I: *This image is a work of a U.S. Army soldier or employee, taken or made as part of that person's official duties. As a work of the U.S. federal government, the image is in the public domain*

[xii] By Cushing Memorial Library and Archives, Texas A&M - Flickr: IBM Processing Machine, CC BY 2.0, https://commons.wikimedia.org/w/index.php?curid=17397582

[xiii] Photo from Museum of LEO Computers Society

[xiv] By ESA, CC BY-SA 3.0-igo

[xv] By National Aeronautics and Space Administration. - http://gimp-savvy.com/cgi-bin/img.cgi?ailsxmzVhD8OjEo694; originally uploaded by Bayo

[xvi] By Lawrence Livermore National Laboratory, Attribution, https://commons.wikimedia.org/w/index.php?curid=1565787

[xvii] PDP-8: This work has been released into the **public domain** by its author, Alkivar at Wikipedia

[xviii] By Jitze Couperus - Flickr: Supercomputer - The Beginnings, CC BY 2.0, https://commons.wikimedia.org/w/index.php?curid=19382150

[xix] Cray I: Clemens PFEIFFER: licensed under the Creative Commons Attribution-Share Alike 2.5 Generic license

[xx] Commodore PET: Rama & Musée Bolo: This work is free software licensed under the Creative Commons Attribution-Share Alike 2.0 France license.

[xxi] IBM PC 5150: Rama & Musée Bolo: This work is free software licensed under the Creative Commons Attribution-Share Alike 2.0 France license.

[xxii] By Blake Patterson from Alexandria, VA, USA - Newton and iPhone: ARM and ARM, CC BY 2.0, https://commons.wikimedia.org/w/index.php?curid=7039806

[xxiii] IBM Simon: Bcos47: The copyright holder of this work, released the work into the **public domain**

[xxiv] Palm TX: Stefano Palazzo: Permission granted to copy, distribute and/or modify this document under the terms of the **GNU Free Documentation License**, Version 1.2 or any later version published by the Free Software Foundation;

[xxv] By Maurizio Pesce from Milan, Italia - OnePlus One vs LG G3 vs Apple iPhone 6 Plus vs Samsung Galaxy Note 4, CC BY 2.0, https://commons.wikimedia.org/w/index.php?curid=46026497

[xxvi] Copied from Official Apple Support

[xxvii] Intel 80486DX CPU. Bottom view with gold plated pins ---- Photograph © Andrew Dunn, 9 November 2005. This file is licensed under the Creative Commons Attribution-Share Alike 2.0 Generic license.

[xxviii] By No machine-readable author provided. Cyberdex assumed (based on copyright claims). - No machine-readable source provided. Own work assumed (based on copyright claims)., Public Domain, https://commons.wikimedia.org/w/index.php?curid=647267

[xxix] Hard Drive; Author: Evan-Amos; This file is licensed under the Creative Commons Attribution-Share Alike 3.0 Unported license

[xxx] Optical Disk; Author: Ubern00b; Permission is granted to copy, distribute and/or modify this document under the terms of the **GNU Free Documentation License**, Version 1.2 or any later version

[xxxi] SanDisk Cruzer Micro; Author: Evan-Amos; The copyright holder of this work has released this work into the **public domain.**

[xxxii] Typing example.ogv. Modifications made by Parzi. This file is licensed under the Creative Commons Attribution-Share Alike 3.0 Unported license

[xxxiii] Tastenmaus von Microsoft; Author: Darkone; This file is licensed under the Creative Commons Attribution-Share Alike 2.5 Generic license

xxxiv TFT_LCD_display_Samsung_SyncMaster_510N.jpg: Author: MaGioZal; This work is free software; you can redistribute it and/or modify it under the terms of the **GNU General Public License** as published by the Free Software Foundation; either version 2 of the License, or any later version

xxxv HP LaserJet 5 printer; Author: Thiemo Schuff; This file is licensed under the Creative Commons Attribution-Share Alike 3.0 Germany license

xxxvi Motherboard; Author: Julianprescott2604juuly; This file is licensed under the Creative Commons Attribution-Share Alike 4.0 International license

xxxvii CPU; Author: Andrew Dunn; This file is licensed under the Creative Commons Attribution-Share Alike 2.0 Generic license

xxxviii CPU Block Diagram; Author: Lambtron; This file is licensed under the Creative Commons Attribution-Share Alike 4.0 International license

xxxix Clock Generator; Author: Audrius Meskauskas Audriusa; This file is licensed under the Creative Commons Attribution-Share Alike 3.0 Unported license

xl "Hard drive-en" by I, Surachit. Licensed under CC BY-SA 3.0 via Commons

xli Typing example.ogv. Modifications made by Parzi. This file is licensed under the Creative Commons Attribution-Share Alike 3.0 Unported license

xlii Punched card: Author: Arnold Reinhold; This file is licensed under the Creative Commons Attribution-Share Alike 2.5 Generic license

xliii Tastenmaus von Microsoft; Author: Darkone; This file is licensed under the Creative Commons Attribution-Share Alike 2.5 Generic license

xliv Scanner; Author: Luke Launderville; This work is licensed under the Creative Commons Attribution-ShareAlike 3.0 License

xlv Capacitive touchscreen of a mobile phone; Author: Medvedev; This file is licensed under the Creative Commons Attribution 3.0 Unported license

xlvi An Internet kiosk in Hemer, Germany; Author: Asio otus; This file is licensed under the Creative Commons Attribution-Share Alike 3.0 Unported license

xlvii Speakers for notebook computers; Author: Evan-Amos; this work was released into the **public domain**

xlviii Headphones; Author: Adamantios; This file is licensed under the Creative Commons Attribution-Share Alike 3.0 Unported, 2.5 Generic, 2.0 Generic and 1.0 Generic license

xlix In-ear headphones; Author: Ballerinus; This file is licensed under the Creative Commons Attribution-Share Alike 3.0 Unported license

l Flat Panel Display; Author: Freeware-flo; Permission is granted to copy, distribute and/or modify this document under the terms of the **GNU Free Documentation License**, Version 1.2 or any later version

li Projector; Author: Michael Movchin; This file is licensed under the Creative Commons Attribution-Share Alike 3.0 Unported license

lii HP LaserJet 5 printer; Author: Thiemo Schuff; This file is licensed under the Creative Commons Attribution-Share Alike 3.0 Germany license

liii Bluetooth mobile phone headset; Author: ed g2s • talk; This file is licensed under the Creative Commons Attribution-Share Alike 3.0 Unported license

liv Maria Toutoudaki/Stockbyte/Getty Images

lv By Pratyeka - Own work, CC BY-SA 4.0, https://commons.wikimedia.org/w/index.php?curid=54659127

[lvi] By Rama & Musée Bolo - Own work, CC BY-SA 2.0 fr, https://commons.wikimedia.org/w/index.php?curid=36769003

[lvii] By unknown, https://en.wikipedia.org/w/index.php?curid=1016513

[lviii] By Screenshot is taken and uploaded by Tyomitch (talk · contribs), https://en.wikipedia.org/w/index.php?curid=2611871

[lix] GPL, https://commons.wikimedia.org/w/index.php?curid=1191127

[lx] By Developers.android.com - https://developer.android.com/design/media/index_landing_page.png, CC BY 2.5, https://commons.wikimedia.org/w/index.php?curid=20780279

[lxi] By www.apple.com, https://en.wikipedia.org/w/index.php?curid=51694141

[lxii] By DigiBarn Computer Museum - www.digibarn.com, CC BY 3.0, https://commons.wikimedia.org/w/index.php?curid=3276768

[lxiii] By DigiBarn Computer Museum - www.digibarn.com, CC BY 3.0, https://commons.wikimedia.org/w/index.php?curid=3276768

[lxiv] By Julianprescott2604juuly - Own work, CC BY-SA 4.0, https://commons.wikimedia.org/w/index.php?curid=38794746

[lxv] CC BY-SA 2.0, https://commons.wikimedia.org/w/index.php?curid=406963

[lxvi] By No machine-readable author provided. Cyberdex assumed (based on copyright claims). - No machine-readable source provided. Own work assumed (based on copyright claims)., Public Domain, https://commons.wikimedia.org/w/index.php?curid=647267

[lxvii] CMOS Battery on a Computer Motherboard. © Steve Gschmeissner / Science Photo Library / Getty Images

[lxviii] Ports on the back of an Apple Mac Mini
Evan-Amos - Own work
Public Domain

[lxix] Typing example.ogv. Modifications made by Parzi. This file is licensed under the Creative Commons Attribution-Share Alike 3.0 Unported license

[lxx] By Drawn by Mysid in CorelDRAW. - Own work, CC BY-SA 3.0, https://commons.wikimedia.org/w/index.php?curid=364930

[lxxi] Public Domain, https://commons.wikimedia.org/w/index.php?curid=874943

[lxxii] Canon CanoScan N 650U Image Scanner. This is an example of a flatbed reflective scanner
By Luke Launderville - I created this work entirely by myself., CC BY-SA 3.0, https://en.wikipedia.org/w/index.php?curid=19637143
This image is licensed under the Creative Commons Attribution-ShareAlike 3.0 License.

[lxxiii] By Chris Whytehead, Chris's Acorns – CC-BY-SA-3.0, CC BY-SA 3.0, https://commons.wikimedia.org/w/index.php?curid=18033660

[lxxiv] By Creative Tools from Halmdstad, Sweden - CreativeTools.se - VIUscan - Laser-scanned - ZPrinter - 3D printed - Viking Belt Buckle 24, CC BY 2.0, https://commons.wikimedia.org/w/index.php?curid=12419129

[lxxv] By Zuzu (Own work) [CC BY-SA 3.0 (http://creativecommons.org/licenses/by-sa/3.0) or GFDL (http://www.gnu.org/copyleft/fdl.html)], via Wikimedia Commons

[lxxvi] Tastenmaus von Microsoft; Author: Darkone; This file is licensed under the Creative Commons Attribution-Share Alike 2.5 Generic license

[lxxvii] By Suimasentyottohensyuushimasuyo - Own work, CC BY-SA 3.0, https://commons.wikimedia.org/w/index.php?curid=1509949

[lxxviii] By Cyrotux - Own work, CC BY-SA 3.0, https://commons.wikimedia.org/w/index.php?curid=2696533

[lxxix] Flat Panel Display; Author: Freeware-flo; Permission is granted to copy, distribute and/or modify this document under the terms of the **GNU Free Documentation License**, Version 1.2 or any later version

[lxxx] By Jari Laamanen - Own work, FAL, https://commons.wikimedia.org/w/index.php?curid=1829066

[lxxxi] By Septagram at English Wikipedia - Transferred from en.wikipedia to Commons by Liftarn using CommonsHelper., Public Domain, https://commons.wikimedia.org/w/index.php?curid=12137116

[lxxxii] By Michael Movchin - Own work, CC BY-SA 3.0, https://commons.wikimedia.org/w/index.php?curid=21150893

[lxxxiii] By Evan-Amos - Own work, Public Domain, https://commons.wikimedia.org/w/index.php?curid=62084213

[lxxxiv] By KDS4444 - Own work, CC BY-SA 4.0, https://commons.wikimedia.org/w/index.php?curid=47285674

[lxxxv] By Fourohfour - Own work, CC BY-SA 2.5, https://commons.wikimedia.org/w/index.php?curid=596036

[lxxxvi] By Original uploaded by Pointillist (Transfered by Gavin.perch) - Original uploaded on en.wikipedia, CC BY-SA 3.0, https://commons.wikimedia.org/w/index.php?curid=13654118

[lxxxvii] By http://muzyczny.pl - http://muzyczny.pl, CC BY-SA 4.0-3.0-2.5-2.0-1.0, https://commons.wikimedia.org/w/index.php?curid=15232513

[lxxxviii] This photo was taken by Evan-Amos as a part of Vanamo Media, which creates public domain works for educational purposes

[lxxxix] By Evan-Amos - Own work, Public Domain, https://commons.wikimedia.org/w/index.php?curid=39729457

[xc] By Original: Evan-Amos Derivative work: Beao - This file was derived from: Usb-thumb-drive.jpg, Public Domain, https://commons.wikimedia.org/w/index.php?curid=12862548

[xci] By George Chernilevsky - Own work, Public Domain, https://commons.wikimedia.org/w/index.php?curid=6963942

[xcii] By Daniel P. B. Smith. - Image by Daniel P. B. Smith.;, CC BY-SA 3.0, https://commons.wikimedia.org/w/index.php?curid=7097264

[xciii] By TedColes - Own work, Public Domain, https://commons.wikimedia.org/w/index.php?curid=11736857

[xciv] By Arnold Reinhold - I took this picture of an artifact in my possession. The card was created in the late 1960s or early 1970s and has no copyright notice., CC BY-SA 2.5, https://commons.wikimedia.org/w/index.php?curid=775153

[xcv] By Morn - Own work, CC BY-SA 3.0, https://commons.wikimedia.org/w/index.php?curid=30135961

[xcvi] By Baran Ivo - Own work, Public Domain, https://commons.wikimedia.org/w/index.php?curid=2964670